Leslie: Triumphs of Identity, Success, And Love

Les Adelson

Dedication

This book is dedicated to my father, Arthur. Through his tireless efforts to provide his family with a home and his tenacity to overcome every obstacle he confronted, he showed me the true value of education and hard work. He loved me unconditionally and had unwavering confidence in me, supporting me every step of the way during his short but meaningful life. He was my best friend and my true inspiration to seek and realize success in finding the true meaning of a life well-lived.

Acknowledgment

There are too many mentors in my life to name and mention them all adequately. They all knew who they were at pivotal moments in my life, and those still on this earth know who they are now and the role they played in shaping me into the man I am today. A special thank you to my dear friends who have listened to my stories over the years and urged me to write this book. And to my friend Mary Ann, thank you for your inspiration in designing the book cover. To the love of my life, Thomas, I thank you for 53 years filled with love, laughter, and happiness beyond comprehension. Our enduring love for one another was boundless and everlasting. I miss you terribly, but you are with me for eternity.

Contents

Chapter 1
A Boy's Awakening

From the very beginning, I knew I was different but did not know how or why. As I grew and matured, my differences, which I did not understand, became my strengths and shaped my life's journey.

I was born in Chicago in 1949. I was the second of two boys born to working-class parents in a suburb outside of downtown Chicago. And so my story of love, loss, challenges and success began.

Mom was born in Romania and came to the U.S. through Ellis Island at age 5. Her father was a tailor, and her mother was a seamstress. They owned a dry-cleaning shop where they also did tailoring and lived in the back of the store with her middle sibling, Dorothy, and youngest sibling brother, Jack. They struggled as all immigrant families did in the 1920's.

My mother always wanted to be a nurse, but my patriarchal grandfather said he would not allow his daughter to see naked men or change bedpans. So she became a cosmetologist, hair, make-up, and nails. My mother confessed to me when I was in my teens that she married my dad (who later became my idol and role model) at age 23 because he was the only one who asked her. But they truly grew to love each other deeply, almost like an arranged marriage. My dad idolized my mother, and my mother "settled" for my dad. He was just an average guy recently discharged from the Army, with no special talents (that she saw) and could only provide her with a simple lifestyle unlike that of her younger sister's upscale life that was made possible by her marriage to a young doctor. She was a homemaker, and we lived in a modest second-floor, two-bedroom apartment.

My father was of Lithuanian heritage and was born and raised in Chicago. He used to say that he graduated from the school of hard knocks. His father died when he was five, and my paternal grandmother ended up in a sanatorium — I'm still not sure what that was all about, but I know that she had shock treatments, and we weren't supposed to talk about her. Without parents, my dad's family decided to adopt his sister but put my dad in an orphanage. Mind you, these were the days when orphanages were like the book Oliver. My dad was beaten, starved, and lived on potatoes, but somehow survived long enough to escape and live on his own by his wit and ability to bullshit anyone. To this day, I don't know how he did it. He never finished high school, but he was the smartest, most clever, independent, and innovative man I ever knew.

I was smart enough to watch him closely and learn from him how to navigate life, which was a real struggle for me. I also felt that we had a lot in common and were bound by our respective struggles. I adored him. As an adult, I called him every day, and we ended every phone call with "I love you." He had no status or class and had to fend for himself. I could write an entire book about my dad, who tragically died at the young age of 67 from a disease he picked up from a lung spore while helping a friend build a house on his friend's property. To cut to the chase, my dad was a janitor, a foreman, and a salesman (he could sell mud to farmers) and educated himself by asking questions and bullshitting and ended up managing 14 high- rise office buildings in West Los Angeles. I was so proud of him. I still miss him and talk to him every day.

My childhood fear of the world, which seemed to deepen with each passing year, found its roots in a traumatic incident that scarred my young psyche when I was just four years old. Our apartment in Chicago, our sanctuary, was violated by intruders, shattering the illusion of safety and security that every child deserves. I can still visualize my mom standing frozen in the living room, crying with disbelief. The memory of that fateful break-in etched itself into my mind like a vivid, recurring nightmare.

I never felt entirely safe again after that incident. The once-familiar sounds of the apartment at night became a source of anxiety. Each creak of a floorboard was a haunting reminder of that intrusion, a chilling echo of the past that sent shivers down my spine. The gust of wind against the windowpane would set my heart racing, as I couldn't help but wonder if "they" were back. That feeling of vulnerability and fear was a relentless specter that cast a long shadow over my childhood, leaving me in a state of constant vigilance.

As a result, my home, which should have been a refuge, felt like a battleground between my desire for safety and my fear of the unknown. The sense of security I so desperately craved remained elusive, and the trauma of that break-in shaped my perception of the world. It left me with a profound and lasting sense of unease, a fear that never truly subsided, even as I grew older.

My life took a huge change the year I turned five when my family made the monumental choice to leave Chicago behind and begin afresh in the golden state of California. My mother, spurred by a desire to be closer to her sister, who had already begun her own journey in California, felt that this country of opportunity carried the promise of a better life, one in which employment was more plentiful and the horizon spread further. However, the reality of California wasn't quite the rosy picture we had imagined.

The transition was challenging, and as we settled into our new life, it became evident that my parents were struggling to keep a roof over our heads. The perceived abundance of opportunities was, for us, elusive, and the dream of a better life felt like it was slipping away. We found ourselves navigating a different set of challenges in a new place, a stark contrast to the life we had known in Chicago. However, our strong family bond with our extended family was the glue that kept us together during these hard times.

My maternal grandmother unexpectedly passed away in Chicago in 1955. This was a shocking event that rocked my family to the core. After her passing, my grandfather decided to move to California and join our family, where he could retire and have a home. He put up the downpayment for a modest home in a middle-class suburb of Los Angeles and moved in with the four of us. He continued to be the patriarch of the family until he remarried several years later and moved out.

What he had left was a new home in which my brother and I could thrive as my dad continued to pursue meaningful and steady employment. Mom loved puttering around her home, gardening, painting walls, etc. but soon decided she needed to get a job to help out financially as my father's job prospects were elusive. My uncle, the doctor and her brother-in-law, gave her a job as an assistant in his medical practice. That helped the family finances immensely. I was never aware that we were poor because I was still in elementary school, but my brother, four years my elder, was keenly aware and was jealous of all the goodies his friends had.

As we settled into our new home, my brother's role as both a protector and a guiding force in my life became even more pronounced. Our sibling connection evolved into a source of strength and support that would shape my formative years.

He went even further, purchasing a pair of boxing gloves for me, a symbolic gesture of his commitment to my protection. He wanted to ensure that I could stand my ground, even in a world that often seemed unkind and unforgiving. His support extended beyond sports, fostering a sense of strength and self-reliance within me.

As "latchkey" kids in our new California neighborhood, my brother took on the role of both a guide and a friend. He would often take me with him when he visited his friends, allowing me to be part of a social circle that would have otherwise remained out of reach. We'd play games and spend time with his friends, bridging the gap between our different age groups. It was a gesture of inclusion that made me feel like an integral part of his world, reinforcing the bond between us.

My brother's kindness and protective instincts became my support during those early years in California. He recognized that I was different, and instead of distancing himself or making me feel like an outcast, he chose to embrace and nurture our sibling relationship.

Michael was not just a protective sibling; he was my confidant and mentor. With infinite patience, he attempted to share his interests with me. When he introduced me to the world of sports, he did it with a sense of purpose. His goal was not only to teach me how to play softball or swing a tennis racket but also to help me feel comfortable among my peers. He knew that these shared activities were gateways to acceptance and camaraderie with other children in our neighborhood. His guidance was a testament to his love, and his support was the foundation on which I could begin to build my self esteem.

Michael was a force to be reckoned with from the very beginning. His brilliance was evident as he tackled advanced calculus in high school. In the realm of academia, he was nothing short of extraordinary, leaving a trail of admiration in his wake. His academic prowess was a testament to the power of his intellect.

What made Michael truly exceptional was the fact that he was not just a scholar but a multifaceted individual. His mind, so sharp in the classroom, was equally at home on the sports field. He was a gifted athlete, seamlessly blending his academic and physical competence. This dual excellence marked him as an all-around exceptional person, a rare breed.

In the eyes of our teachers and classmates, Michael was more than a student; he was a role model. He was an embodiment of excellence that set the bar for all of us. His talents and accomplishments were legendary within the walls of our school. As his younger sibling, I couldn't help but grapple with a starkly different self-perception. Michael's brilliance cast a long shadow, one that seemed impossible to escape. In the eyes of others, my own accomplishments felt inconsequential compared to his towering achievements. I was constantly measured against the yardstick of his success.

The weight of my insecurities became a heavy burden to bear. My interests diverged from Michael's path. While he excelled in academics and sports, I found my refuge in the world of arts and social engagement. The chorus, the thrill of acting in plays, and the joy of participating in social committees were my chosen domains. These activities held a special place in my heart, nurturing my unique talents and offering me a sense of belonging.

The constant reminder of my brother's academic success came not only from my peers but from teachers who had also taught him. Their incredulous expressions, the recurrent "I can't believe you're Michael's brother," served as a relentless undercurrent in my academic and social life. It was as though his legacy had preordained my identity. The secret that I would not discover until I became a teenager was that Michael, too, was insecure and needy.

My parents were blue collar laborers when we were kids. To maintain a roof over our heads and food on the table, they were doing their utmost. Michael was envious of his friends who had automobiles, went on family vacations, and had a boat they could use on rivers. Because of his friendships with wealthier individuals, Michael participated in several events with the family of a specific friend, Larry. He was able to enjoy leisure pursuits like boating and mountain climbing while on vacation with Larry and his family.

Michael started taking every job he could to make enough money to acquire the things he enjoyed and desired. As a teenager and in later years, he had many jobs and professions. He drove an ambulance, performed retail sales, worked in an emergency call center, and was a bus boy, bag boy, bar tender, and barista.

However, his career as a flight attendant significantly altered this his life.

He had suffered injuries from severe turbulence during a trip while he was employed with an airline. Because of all the bending and reaching throughout that voyage, he got to know coworkers who suffered from the same neck and back problems.

A large number of flight attendants, he would learn, saw a chiropractor for their ailments. This treatment not only helped him with his job related injuries, but became a career that he would later embrace and master as a successful chiropractor himself.

What made matters even more challenging for me growing up was my name, Leslie. In a world where names often carry certain expectations and stereotypes, my name was a source of constant frustration. Leslie, a name that held no distinction of gender, was a double-edged sword, it made me an easy target for bullying, both from peers and, surprisingly, even from some teachers.

At one point in my life, at age 12, I told my mother that I wanted to change my name to David. As customary in Jewish families, children are named for a relative after they pass. I told her that I hated my name, but when she told me about the person behind my name and how my namesake great uncle was a wonderful and successful man, I felt proud. She also pointed out successful men in the world whose name was Leslie. So I decided to accept it.

However, in a society where names often come with predefined gender roles and expectations, Leslie stood apart as an anomaly. It neither leaned toward the traditionally masculine nor the feminine and this very fluidity, while liberating in some respects, also created a breeding ground for confusion and judgment. My name became a symbol of my struggle to fit into the rigid molds society prescribed.

The significance of my name became glaringly evident during one of the most frustrating incidents I faced in my early years. To my surprise and dismay, I found myself placed in girl's physical education classes or summoned to the girl's vice principal's office solely because of my name. The misjudgment was as hurtful as it was bewildering. The assumption that my name defined my gender was a sharp and painful reminder of the preconceived notions that surrounded me. The experience left me feeling misunderstood, mislabeled, and deeply alienated.

Classmates were quick to seize upon this opportunity to taunt and jeer. The words and laughter of my peers became a cruel echo, a continuous reminder that my identity was not mine to define. I became a target, not because of who I was, but because of a name over which I had no control. The irony of the situation was inescapable. My name embodied the essence of who I truly was.

My struggles to assert my identity and escape the imposing shadow of my brother seemed to compound with each passing day. It was a tumultuous time marked by questions of self-worth and the constant battle to be recognized for who I was rather than being judged based on arbitrary criteria. The weight of the world's expectations, coupled with my name's neutrality, pushed me to steer through a complex terrain of identity, one where I would ultimately have to fight to define myself on my terms. However, I always kept with me the words of wisdom, perhaps a premonition of what was to come, that my mother gave me when she wrote the following in my elementary school graduation autograph book:

"Your life ahead will be filled with many bumps in the road and unexpected twists and turns, but you, my dear, will surmount them all and be a successful man."

Throughout my elementary and middle school years, I found solace and purpose in being an active participant in various committees and planning activities. The world of student governance became a place where I could channel my energy and creativity. I ran for student council offices, sometimes winning and sometimes losing, but each experience became a stepping stone in my journey of self discovery and empowerment. These early forays into leadership gave me a sense of purpose and an outlet for my passion.

It wasn't until I reached middle school that a significant change occurred in my life. I began going by the name "Les," a suggestion I received from a teacher who, I believe, was trying to protect me from the challenges posed by my given name, Leslie. This adjustment marked a pivotal moment in my exploration of identity. It was an early step in acknowledging that I was different in ways I didn't fully understand at the time.

I was at an age when I didn't have a clear understanding of my own identity or the complexities of human attraction. I couldn't say that I was attracted to boys, but I knew I liked looking at them. In contrast, I cherished the company of girls and enjoyed activities like shopping and dancing that were often associated with female socialization. I reveled in the affection and camaraderie that my female friends offered. I never felt a desire to become a girl, dress like one, or mimic their behavior, but I cherished the deep connections and shared experiences that came from these friendships. My world was predominantly female, and I found comfort and acceptance among my friends, who supported and encouraged my individuality.

I was often at odds with the world's expectations, a feeling that permeated my daily life and shaped my sense of self. The struggle to break free from the boxes society tried to place me in was a constant battle, one that challenged my very essence and compelled me to assert my individuality.

The world had its preconceived notions and stereotypes, often driven by conventional norms and expectations. From an early age, I was keenly aware that I didn't neatly fit into the molds that society had crafted. My interests, my unconventional name, and the perceptions of my abilities compared to my accomplished brother all served as reminders that I was seen through a particular lens.

The pressure to conform to these expectations was unrelenting. It seemed as though the world had set a predefined path for me, one that didn't align with my true self. This internal conflict, the friction between who I was and who the world expected me to be, became a defining feature of my voyage.

The struggle to break free was an emotional one, marked by moments of self-doubt, frustration, and a longing to be understood for who I truly was. I was determined not to be limited by the constraints of tradition or the judgments of others. This determination became the driving force behind my resolve to carve my unique identity to transcend the boxes that society tried to place me in.

With each challenge, whether it was the misjudgment of my name, the teasing from peers, or the doubts of educators, I drew strength from the belief that I could chart my own course. I was determined to prove that my identity was not confined to the expectations of others. I was an individual with my own dreams, desires, and potential, and I was resolute in my determination to break free from the limitations imposed by society's expectations.

This ongoing battle against conformity and the quest for self expression would continue to shape my journey, serving as a testament to the power of resilience and the enduring human spirit. It was a testament to the belief that, regardless of the boxes society tried to place us in, we possess the capacity to break free and define our own destinies.

Despite the emotional and identity challenges I faced, I discovered a unique expertise within myself during my formative years. I was inherently innovative and displayed a natural entrepreneurial spirit. My parents' financial limitations meant that if I wanted something, I had to find a way to get it. I embraced the art of resourcefulness and went door to door selling everything from seeds to Christmas cards. I would do whatever it took to earn enough money or 'points' to attain the items I desired, such as a bicycle or a coveted toy. This early drive for independence and self-sufficiency marked the beginning of my ambition towards self-reliance.

The age of 16 marked yet another turning point in my life, an age when I seized an opportunity that would redefine my educational journey and pave the way for a future of my own making. I enrolled in a work experience program, which, in many ways, was a pivotal declaration of my independence and determination to chart a course that defied the expectations that had been imposed upon me.

The decision to change my major from college prep to general education was not taken lightly. It meant diverging from the conventional path that society and my family had laid out for me. High school guidance counselors often suggested that I wasn't cut out for college and that I should take a vocational track instead. The pressure to conform to these expectations was relentless, and it could have easily stifled my aspirations. However, somewhere deep within me, I held an unwavering belief that I was intelligent, and I was determined to prove all those who doubted me wrong.

This new freedom to work during school hours gave me the opportunity to accumulate summer school credits as well. This shift allowed me to graduate from high school at age 17, earlier than expected. It was a significant achievement, one that signified not just academic progress but a profound transformation in my self worth.

This period of my life was a metamorphosis, a time when I shed the doubts and insecurities that had held me back for so long. The challenges I had faced—the emotional turmoil of being compared to my accomplished brother, the struggles imposed by a name that defied convention, and the responsibilities of financial independence—became the stepping stones on my path to self discovery and resilience.

I was no longer content to conform to the narratives others had written for me. Instead, I was determined to carve out my unique identity. This journey was not just about proving myself to others; it was about proving to myself that success was not bound by convention. It was about acknowledging that my potential was limited only by the boundaries I chose to set for myself.

The difficulties I encountered in my formative years became the very fuel that ignited my determination to rise above them. I had an unwavering belief in my own intelligence and potential, a belief that remained steadfast even when others doubted me.

The more people questioned my abilities or tried to fit me into predetermined roles, the more determined I became to prove them wrong.

This pursuit of success was not merely about achieving recognition or accolades; it was a deeply ingrained desire to prove that I could overcome all the odds stacked against me. It became a matter of personal pride, a fierce commitment to demonstrate my worth and capabilities in a world that often seemed intent on underestimating me.

My belief in my own potential, coupled with my determination to challenge societal expectations, fueled my inner fire. It became the driving force behind my life's journey, propelling me to rise above challenges and carve my own unique path. I was resolved to show that I could not only overcome adversity but also make a meaningful impact in a world that sometimes struggled to understand or accept my differences.

Chapter 2
Navigating a Hostile World

My life was intricate and multifaceted, marked by the struggle to understand and accept my own sexuality. I didn't recognize or acknowledge my sexuality until college, and during my childhood and early teens, the negative feedback I received often manifested as mocking name-calling and a general sense of confusion about who I was. These experiences were emotionally challenging as I grappled with societal norms and struggled to reconcile my identity with the expectations placed upon me.

One distinct memory that lingers is that of Barry, a friend of my brother's, who attempted to guide me in walking more "manly." He pointed out that I took shorter steps and walked in a way he perceived as effeminate. His well-intentioned advice, though misguided, became a reflection of the broader social pressures that weighed on me. In response, I took his advice to heart and actively worked on altering my gait. Throughout my teenage years, I remained acutely aware of my walk, often feeling self-conscious about it.

As I entered college, the environment became more open-minded and accepting. I was no longer subjected to the same degree of judgment and stereotyping that I had experienced earlier in life. However, my own self-acceptance and the act of coming out as gay presented a new emotional challenge. While I was surrounded by friends who were more understanding and supportive, I chose to keep my feelings private, a reflection of the residual fears and insecurities that had been ingrained in me.

It was a momentous decision to reveal my true self to my closest friends. I remember when I decided to tell them I was gay. It was a daunting and emotionally charged experience. I shared this truth one friend at a time, and each disclosure brought with it a mix of anxiety and anticipation. The emotional weight of the secret I had carried for so long was palpable.

In response to my revelation, my friends exhibited remarkable respect and love. They welcomed me with open arms, embracing me for who I truly was. The acceptance I found in their reactions was a profound and emotional experience, one that filled the void I had felt for so long.

One of my friends, in particular, played a pivotal role in my journey of self-discovery. Judy, who was a part of this supportive group, revealed that she, too, was gay. Her guidance, mentorship, and friendship became a lifeline as I navigated the complexities of my emerging gay identity.

Judy, who was four years older than me, was my confidante and guide in the realm of gay life, played a pivotal role in my changing my life. She introduced me to a world I had long kept hidden, a world of gay bars and social circles that felt like a vibrant and authentic reflection of who I was. Her mentorship extended beyond mere introductions; she even taught me how to dance with a man and flirt, skills that felt foreign yet empowering.

Our experiences were separate from our school life and our mutual friends. During our college years, we continued to party and have fun with them, but we were not out, with the exception of our close-knit circle. The 1960s was a unique time in history, with growing openness and acceptance of LGBTQ+ individuals, yet the shadows of discrimination and stigma still loomed large. For Judy and me, living two lives was the reality due to the complexities of our dual identities.

Eventually, years later, I mustered the courage to reveal our secret identities to other friends outside of our inner-circle. It was a moment fraught with anxiety and fear as I unveiled what I had once considered a "horrible secret." I braced myself for their reactions, expecting judgment or alienation. To my immense surprise, however, all of my friends found it to be a non-issue and were saddened that I hadn't been able to be myself with them for so many years.

This revelation transformed our friendships, deepening the bonds we had nurtured for so long. Some of my friends expressed hurt at not having been trusted with this information earlier, emphasizing that it wouldn't have changed a thing in their acceptance of us. Others were saddened by the fact that we had suffered in silence for so long, and they expressed remorse that our "secret" had been so difficult.

From that point forward, we were completely out within and outside of our circle of friends. Tom, who had been my partner in secrecy, now participated in all our get-togethers and adventures with open authenticity. Judy, who did not have a partner at the time, joined us as well. She maintained her privacy regarding her love life as she was involved with one of our professors, and the circumstances prevented her from revealing that aspect of her identity.

The acceptance, love, and understanding that flowed from my friends was an emotional revelation, proving that sometimes the weight of our own fears and self-doubt can be heavier than the reality of others' acceptance. Our shared path of self-discovery had forged an even stronger bond within our circle of friends, and the relationships we held dear became an unwavering source of support as we embraced our true selves. In the midst of changing times and shifting social norms, our friendships were filled with love, acceptance, and the courage to be authentic.

Tom (who would later become my life partner) and I had embarked on a journey of self-discovery and authenticity of our own, not just within our circle of friends but within ourselves and our families. Tom's parents were aware of his sexuality and accepted him for who he was. It was just a part of him, something they understood and didn't judge. I, on the other hand, had not yet revealed my true self to my parents, and the prospect of doing so filled me with fear and uncertainty. I was exceptionally close to my parents and my brother, and this was my only secret, a deeply personal truth I had yet to share.

The weight of this unspoken truth had grown heavier with each passing day. I knew that I couldn't carry this secret any longer, and I had decided it was time to be honest with my parents.

I remember that counseling session vividly. My parents sat there, puzzled, not knowing why they had been asked to attend. It was a tense and emotionally charged moment. Finally, it was my turn to speak. With a deep breath, I spoke my truth, "I have always shared everything in my life with you, but there is one thing you need to know. I am a homosexual, and I am in a relationship with Tom. We are planning on getting an apartment and moving in together."

My mother's immediate response was, "Is this because of something that I did?" Her question was a reflection of her love and concern for me, but it also carried an underlying fear that, somehow, her actions had led to my sexuality. I was immensely relieved that Mario was there to guide the conversation. He explained to them that homosexuality was not something parents caused or influenced, and he emphasized that it was simply who I was, how I identified, and who I loved.

It was a defining moment when my father disclosed that he had known about my sexuality for a long time. He had overheard my telephone conversations with friends while he was in the den next to my bedroom, watching TV. He hadn't shared this knowledge with my mother and had never confronted me about it. The session concluded with my parents telling me and Mario that they loved me, but they needed time to process.

Coming out to one's parents is often fraught with anxiety and uncertainty. In this deeply emotional moment, as I drove home with my mother and father in the car after our counseling session, the atmosphere was heavy with tension and anticipation. My mother's willingness to learn and understand, to bridge the gap between her existing knowledge and this new revelation, was both heartening and courageous.

Her first question, "Which one of you is the lesbian?" made me burst out laughing with a realization that I had a lot of explaining to do. However, this innocent query, born out of a genuine desire to comprehend, managed to break the ice and diffuse some of the heaviness in the air. Laughter became a bridge, connecting us in that moment and helping to ease the emotional burden.

Upon arriving home, my father's words had a profound impact. "You are my son, and I will always love you," he declared. It was a simple yet deeply meaningful affirmation of his love and acceptance. For me, it was a moment of immense relief, a weight lifted from my shoulders. The acknowledgement of my identity and the reassurance of his unwavering love filled my heart with gratitude.

In response, I expressed my desire for their love to extend beyond the role of parent and child to encompass the person I truly was. My father's candid response, "I will do my best," was an honest acknowledgment of his commitment to understanding and embracing this new aspect of my identity. His forehead kiss and the words "goodnight" carried profound significance – they signaled not only the end of that day but also the beginning of a deeper connection and understanding between us.

The acceptance of my parents represented an important and transformative turning point in my life. It was not just a single moment but a process that initiated a more open and honest relationship between us. This understanding transcended labels and preconceived notions, reshaping the foundation of our connection.

Revealing to my brother that I was gay was excruciating. I wasn't worried about him accepting me, but I felt that I might be disappointing him. I walked into his apartment and told him that I needed to have a talk with him. It was difficult to get the words out. When I said," I want to tell you that I am gay," he broke into tears. I was so upset. I was certain that this was the end of our relationship.

To my surprise and relief, he looked at me and said, "I am not crying because you are gay, I am crying because I could feel the horrific pain you were in as you tried to tell me. I am so sad that this is difficult for you and that you are suffering." We embraced and he told me that he loved me no matter what.

The journey of self-acceptance and coming out is a deeply personal one, often marked by fear, uncertainty, and a longing for validation from those closest to us. I never have, not will I, advocate that gay men and women should come out to friends and family.

Everyone's situation is different. This is a personal decision that can only be made by each individual. Our personal life experiences and situations dictate what we need to do for ourselves.

The pivotal role of my parents in this journey cannot be overstated. Their love and support provided the emotional bedrock I needed to navigate the challenges ahead.

This acceptance was not just about my sexual orientation; it was a validation of my identity as a whole. It reaffirmed that my parents loved me not for any preconceived idea of who I should be but for the person I truly was. This reassurance helped me get past the wounds of rejection and misunderstanding I had experienced in the past.

Through their acceptance, my parents demonstrated that love and understanding could triumph over fear and prejudice. They offered hope, not just for me but for countless others who grapple with their identities and the fear of rejection. Their willingness to embrace and support me allowed me to be true to myself, unburdened by the weight of secrecy or self-doubt.

It was a powerful lesson in the capacity of love to transcend societal norms and biases. Their acceptance was a profound testament to the unbreakable bond of family, one that can weather the storms of adversity and emerge stronger on the other side. It provided the emotional nourishment I needed to continue toward self acceptance and authenticity.

In essence, this turning point was a testament to the enduring power of love, and it served as a catalyst for a more authentic and fulfilling life. It was a reminder that, despite the challenges and prejudices of the world, the support and understanding of those who truly care for us can make all the difference, allowing us to find acceptance within our families and, by extension, within ourselves.

The world for gay men and women was one of protective and separate spheres, with many living dual lives to shield their true identities. However, Tom and I were fortunate to have had very different experiences. Our families were exceptionally accepting, and we were embraced simply as Les and Tom, and to our nieces and nephews, we were Uncle Les and Uncle Tom. Our home was a space where we hosted major celebrations, bringing together our parents, siblings, and nieces and nephews. We would cook, decorate, and share love and laughter, all feeling perfectly normal within the warm embrace of our family.

However, the comfort we enjoyed within our family had to be shed as we stepped out into the world. We weren't universally accepted, and the challenges became most apparent as I pursued a career in education. My dream was to become a teacher, but the reality of being a gay man in a profession that was not always open to such diversity presented obstacles.

By the time I finished college, I had met Tom, and we were in a loving relationship. Still, I kept my personal life hidden from colleagues and acquaintances, even though many found me to be personable and friendly. I was cautious with my pronouns, never openly mentioned doing things together with my friend, and always referred to myself as "I," never "we." Tom's career in the travel industry provided a more accepting environment, and it became clear that being gay was a non-issue in his world.

Securing my first teaching job proved to be more challenging than I had ever anticipated. I don't know if school administrators were passing me by due to my appearance, personal characteristics, or mannerisms, but the search was arduous.

Eventually, I was hired at Oxnard High School, where I taught educationally mentally retarded high school students. The school's student body was predominantly Hispanic, and the kids often spoke in Spanish among themselves. While my students seemed to like and respect me, there was an undercurrent of mockery behind my back, with some of them using the term "maricon," which translates to homosexual and is considered a derogatory slur. The teachers and principal appeared to like me, but there was a noticeable absence of deep connections.

The turning point came after a student struck me after I referred him to the office for discipline. He was eventually expelled, but the aftermath of that incident was unsettling. I began receiving death threats from random students, leaving me paralyzed with fear.

Oftentimes, intimidating individuals would approach me,

saying, "Adelson, you're dead." The situation had escalated to the point where I had to have a school security officer meet me at my car in the morning as I arrived on campus and then escort me back to it after school. I'm not entirely sure how I managed, but I summoned the strength to finish my term and then left the school district.

Thankfully, my experience in the Oxnard High School district did not define the rest of my teaching career. I was able to secure teaching jobs in various settings, leveraging my experience and earning excellent references. Throughout my teaching career, I worked with students of all ages, from elementary to middle and high school, in both general education and special education. The challenges I faced early in my career served as a reminder of the obstacles overcome, further strengthening my resolve to advocate for equality and acceptance, both within and beyond the classroom.

A significant turning point in my life revealed itself through an unexpected friendship with a colleague. One of the teachers at the school where I taught, Shari, had developed a fondness for me and started to become more personal in her interactions. We happened to live near each other, and we made the decision to carpool to school, a drive of approximately 45 minutes each way. During these long drives to and from school, Shari and I formed a deep and genuine friendship. Still, I had not yet revealed anything about Tom or my sexuality. It was an unspoken part of my life, concealed beneath the surface.

One day, during our daily carpooling commute, Shari extended an invitation that took me by complete surprise. She said, "My husband and I are having a Sunday brunch at my house, and I would love for you to come, and I'd like you to bring your friend." I was momentarily stunned, but without hesitation, I responded, "Yes, I would love to come, and I know Tom would like it as well." This seemingly ordinary invitation marked the beginning of a remarkable 50-year friendship.

Tom and I attended the brunch, and to my amazement, Shari had also invited another teacher from our school and her husband, who taught at one of the middle schools. It was a wonderful gathering, filled with laughter and shared stories. There was no discussion of "who we were"; we were simply friends, coming together to enjoy each other's company. This brunch became a pivotal moment in my professional coming-out journey, and it seemed that Shari had been the catalyst that brought me out of my self-imposed shell.

In my fifth year of teaching, I found myself at an elementary school, where I taught learning handicapped children in fourth to sixth grade. It was during this period that Anita Bryant initiated her notorious anti-gay crusade, and in California, the Briggs Proposition loomed on the ballot. This proposition aimed to forbid homosexuals from working in various professions, and, most critically, it specifically targeted teachers. It was a frightening and uncertain time, and the fear I lived with was amplified by the proposition's rising popularity and the expectation that it would be approved by the voters.

The challenges I encountered during those years were nothing short of overwhelming. Society's norms and expectations were at odds with my true identity, and the prospect of living authentically in the face of discrimination and prejudice was daunting. The shadow of the Briggs Proposition loomed ominously, threatening to exclude LGBTQ+ individuals from numerous professions, with teachers specifically in its crosshairs. It was a deeply unsettling time for those like me, who were determined to live openly and proudly as our true selves.

In the midst of this adversity, it was the support and acceptance of friends like Shari that became a lifeline. Her invitation to that pivotal brunch was a bridge to a world where acceptance transcended labels and where friendships could flourish without the burden of societal expectations. Through her friendship and the courage she inspired in me, I found the strength to continue my journey toward self acceptance.

During those turbulent times, a seemingly innocuous encounter with a fellow teacher would set into motion a series of events that would both terrify and ultimately empower me. My colleague took me aside, questioning the nature of my relationship with Mrs. C., a name that initially left me bewildered. I responded that everything was fine, confused by her inquiry. She offered only a cryptic warning: "Just be careful when you are around her." This left me utterly perplexed, as my interactions with Mrs. C., whose son John was in my class, had been entirely uneventful, and there was no apparent animosity between us.

Shortly after this disconcerting conversation, I was summoned to meet with the school principal, Marilyn. Marilyn was an outstanding educator, and it was common knowledge that she was a lesbian, even though it was not openly discussed. She had a strong presence and only dressed in pantsuits. Her approach was direct and unapologetic. As I walked into her office, she pulled her chair next to mine, locking eyes with me and stated matter-of-factly, "Look, I know you're gay, and you know I'm gay, so let's just get past that." Her candidness left me flabbergasted. Marilyn proceeded to inform me that Mrs. C. had overheard a conversation at a bowling alley in which my instructional aide, Beverly, had referred to me as gay. I had never explicitly revealed my sexual orientation to Beverly, but she had picked up on the subtle clues. Disturbed by the situation and genuinely concerned for my well-being, the teacher who had previously cautioned me against Mrs. C. decided to share this information with Marilyn.

The timing of these events was incredibly precarious, given that a ballot proposition was underway, one that sought to ban homosexuals from working in education. The fear and anxiety that engulfed me were overwhelming, as I could envision my entire career crumbling before my eyes.

Marilyn assured me that she had a strategy to address the situation effectively. She had already consulted with the superintendent of schools without revealing the identity of the teacher in question, as there were five male teachers in the school at the time. The superintendent's response was critical, as he stated, "We do not have gay teachers in our school district. We may have teachers who are gay, but they are not gay teachers." This response provided a glimmer of hope in a perilous situation.

Marilyn's plan hinged on my silence, particularly regarding my knowledge of the situation. She orchestrated a meeting with Mrs. C., explaining that she had heard rumors being spread about me expressing her concern that this could escalate and damage Mrs.

C.'s reputation. Marilyn deftly shifted the focus to the potential repercussions for all the male teachers, some of whom had families and children, underscoring the potential fallout. In response, Mrs. C. apologized and promised to cease spreading rumors. Marilyn even suggested transferring her son John to another classroom to alleviate her concerns, but Mrs. C. was adamant that John adored me and didn't want any changes.

Although it seemed like the issue had been resolved, the year that followed was filled with anxiety and fear. John remained in my class, and Mrs. C. remained a presence in my life. I attempted to conform to societal expectations of masculinity, stifling my true self. Every encounter with Mrs. C. filled me with dread, making it a challenging and disheartening year. The thought of ending my teaching career crossed my mind, but I couldn't allow Mrs. C. to win by forcing me into hiding. I had too much to offer as an educator, and so I persevered, refusing to succumb to fear.

The school year eventually came to an end, and John moved on to middle school along with his mother. This allowed me to breathe a sigh of relief and regain my sense of professional and personal freedom.

From this ordeal, Marilyn and I forged a lasting friendship. She introduced me to her partner, Claudia, who was a vice principal at one of the middle schools in the same district, and I, in turn, introduced them to Tom. The four of us joined forces in opposing the Proposition that aimed to discriminate against LGBTQ+ individuals. We attended fundraisers and events together, and Marilyn and Claudia introduced us to their circle of friends. It was a transformative period in our lives, as Tom and I found a social circle of like-minded gay men and women, something we had never experienced before. The proposition was defeated!

Chapter 3
Years of Love, Laughter, and Lifelong Commitment

Growing up, I knew I was attracted to men, but I never dared act upon those feelings. Instead, I had a lot of girlfriends and experimented with having sex with girls. I enjoyed it but, something was missing, and I did not know what. Mind you, I was 16, 17, 18; what do any young boys know about lovemaking and sex? I was so responsible, however, that I made sure to take all precautions (even in the back of my brother's VW!) to ensure safety from pregnancy. I saw that happen to too many friends, and I was wise enough to ensure that I did not sideline my life. Finding an older friend to purchase condoms is completely another story.

There was a stage in my life that was complicated by traditional expectations and familial goals. I found myself at the confluence of societal conventions and inner reality after being born into a first- generation European Jewish household.

The script initially followed the well-trodden path: engagement at the tender age of 19 to a charming Jewish girl. Sandy possessed an adoration for me that, at the time, I believed mirrored my own feelings. Yet, a subtle undercurrent of unrest persisted, a nagging feeling that something vital was absent.

I was never comfortable with the engagement and was deeply concerned about the future and felt trapped. However, I stumbled upon a stroke of fortune. The love I sought to provide was not the love she craved. It became apparent to her that something was missing in our relationship. She yearned for more passion while I remained uninterested in finding stolen moments of affection and wanted a quiet night's sleep, mindful of the demands of the approaching workday.

The unspoken relief of our parting was not just a deviation from societal expectations; it was an escape from the intricate complications that ensnared many of my peers. The specter of unhappiness, fractured marriages, and strained family bonds loomed over the lives of those who adhered to convention.

Yet, this chapter in my narrative held a revelation—a truth yet to be unveiled. Beneath the surface of societal expectations and familial traditions, I confronted a reality that had long been obscured. It wasn't a lack of love or commitment that had driven a wedge between us; it was the unspoken truth of my authentic self.

In the span of several months following my broken engagement, my life took an unexpected turn. I found myself entangled in several romantic and sexual escapades with men. It was a time for exploration and confusion. My desperation for approval and a longing for genuine connection led me down a path of self- discovery.

I found myself navigating a maze of emotions and experiences, trying to understand my desires and seeking a connection that went beyond the surface. Engaging in romantic and sexual rendezvous was an attempt to explore my attractions and alleviate my guilt and shame that lingered within me. I craved affection, validation, and a sense of belonging, but beneath it all, a deep-seated insecurity about my self-worth prevailed.

Despite being popular in the straight world, with a vibrant

personality, numerous friends, and a clear roadmap for success, my self-concept was tainted by poor body image, doubts about my intelligence, and an overall sense of fear and inadequacy. I was driven by a need for control, perhaps stemming from a fear of losing myself in the chaotic unpredictability of life.

Then, everything changed when I met the love of my life, setting the stage for a transformative journey that would span 53 years. The initial encounter took place at a social bar in the San Fernando Valley called The Apartment, where I first laid eyes on him. At the time, he was one of the most popular figures in the bar scene, making a grand entrance fashionably late, commanding attention with his striking presence. Despite his popularity, I couldn't stand him. He seemed obnoxious, and my perception was clouded by rumors of his romantic escapades.

Tom, with his 27-inch waist and leather vest over his shirtless torso seemed someone completely foreign to me, Initially, I didn't realize it, but I was jealous of his total self-confidence and acceptance of his lifestyle. He was having the time of his life with admirable joie de vivre. Perhaps that was the thing that put me off.

However, our connection deepened over subsequent meetings, evolving from chance encounters to intentional conversations. The difference of our personalities, once a source of disdain, became the foundation for a unique and complementary partnership.

What had started as a quest for affection and self-discovery now blossomed into a profound and unexpected love story. The contrast between our lives — his freewheeling spirit and my cautious nature— blended seamlessly, creating a harmonious balance that neither of us could have predicted.

During one of our long conversations, a transformation occurred. The insecurities that had haunted me for so long began to dissolve, and were now replaced with confidence and acceptance of both myself and the person I was growing to love.

As I settled into a quiet corner of "The Apartment" on that fateful Wednesday night in the winter of 1970, I was in an overworked and emotionally drained state. I had decided to take my friend Judy's advice and go to The Apartment for a drink. I was seeking a break from the demands of my busy daily life.

Wearing a simple denim work shirt and jeans, far from the meticulously planned outfits of the typical socialite, I hesitated at the entrance. The music and the muted conversations of the few patrons created an atmosphere of solace, a departure from the chaotic energy that often defined such spaces. Despite my initial resistance, I stepped in, seeking a reprieve from the demands of my responsibilities.

To my surprise, the charismatic figure I had once disliked, Tom, was there sans his usual entourage. The absence of the adoring crowd that usually surrounded him transformed the atmosphere, and for the first time, he appeared approachable. We locked eyes, and in that unassuming moment, the dynamics between us began to shift.

As we engaged in conversation, the barriers that had previously separated us crumbled away. Tom's larger-than-life persona faded, revealing a person with depths of vulnerability and authenticity that I had never anticipated. What started as a chance encounter unfolded into a genuine connection, a meeting of two souls at a crossroads in their lives.

Our conversation meandered through the complexities of our individual journeys. Tom's past, once seen through the lens of judgment, now became a narrative of resilience and growth. In turn, I found myself sharing the intricacies of my own struggles, exposing the layers of self-doubt that I had held for far too long.

The unexpected twists of fate and the convergence of our paths on that unassuming Wednesday night set the stage for a love story that would transcend the boundaries of our expectations. This chance meeting would become the prologue to a romance that would define the chapters of my life in ways I had never dared to imagine.

It was as if a veil had been lifted, revealing the real Tom— smart, fun, interesting, and engaging. The stark contrast to the image I had harbored in my mind left me pleasantly shocked. We delved into topics ranging from our pasts to our aspirations, sharing stories and laughter that resonated with a rare authenticity.

As the clock struck 2:00 am and the bar began to close its doors, neither of us was ready to part ways. Tom expressed his surprise at discovering the depth of my character. I couldn't help but reciprocate the sentiment, acknowledging the unexpected connection we had stumbled upon. Laughter echoed between us, a shared appreciation for the twists that life had thrown our way.

Reluctant to let the night end, we decided to continue our conversation in my car in the dimly lit parking lot. As the conversation flowed seamlessly, we lost track of time, engrossed in each other's company until the clock struck 4:00 am.

Reality beckoned; I had a few hours before school and work demanded my attention, while Tom had no timeline. Yet, the connection we had forged was too compelling to let it end. In a bold move, I suggested meeting for dinner one night, a proposition met with an affirmative "yes" from Tom. We exchanged phone numbers and went our separate ways as the night gave way to dawn.

That night, filled with laughter, honesty, and unexpected connection, marked the beginning of a journey that would change our lives in ways I never could have imagined. The universe, it seemed, had orchestrated this serendipitous meeting, setting the stage for what would become a love story.

The weeks that followed were nothing short of magical, marked by a connection that surpassed the physical realm. It felt like the first time I had truly made love, a profound and intimate experience that laid the foundation for the inseparable bond we would share in the days to come.

Our lives became woven together from that day forward, yet the path was far from smooth. At the ages of twenty-one and twenty-four, we were still finding our way in the world. I juggled the demands of college, working tirelessly to obtain my teaching credentials and striving for independence from my parents. Tom, with his background in dog breeding and his past as the breadwinner for his family, faced his own set of challenges.

Thomas Oliver Hall, born in Chicago in 1945, emerged as a kindred spirit. It was uncanny to discover that he was born merely five miles from the hospital where I myself was born. The parallel continued as I learned about the circumstances surrounding his delivery, mirroring the cesarean section that brought me into the world. Was this the Universe in action?

Tom was from a Catholic family of middle European descent and English heritage. Growing up in a household where his grandmother spoke Czech, this became his first language. His journey led him to California at the age of 16, aligning remarkably with my own relocation to the West Coast at the age of 5.

Tom suffered from a rare skin condition that would burn his skin at the slightest intense friction even as a small boy. As a result, he spent much of his early formative years confined to his home. He could not go to school, play with friends, or take long walks without developing terrible blisters on his feet.

Tom's grandmother indulged him and catered to all of his whims because of this illness. He was completely spoiled. Tom was a genius. He was a voracious reader of all kinds of material and a world student who used books, periodicals, and movies to learn about the world.

My roots are traced back to Romania and Lithuania, infusing our lives with shared experiences and a love for European cuisine. It was a delightful revelation to find that our upbringings were mixed with similar cultural nuances that set us apart from the conventional American narrative.

Tom appreciated my Judaism and delighted in the customs of the Jewish festivals, particularly the meals! Our connection was unaffected by our differing religious beliefs. He got more and more Jewish to the point that others began to believe he was Jewish. He spent a number of years working with five Jewish women at a travel firm. He became fluent in Yiddish, to the point that my mother would burst out laughing when he spoke it correctly and utilized all of the idioms.

Tom's life took a turn when his parents separated at the age of 16, prompting a move to California with his sister and grandmother. In a testament to his resilience, they secured a small house in the San Fernando Valley, where his mother, Antionette, worked tirelessly to sustain the family. Tom, at a young age, assumed the role of a major breadwinner. He and his younger sister Suzanne fought for attention. He got along well with his sister, but at sixteen she moved out of the family and married a sailor. Their affection for one another only deepened as adults.

Tom had a unique passion for raising purebred dogs. His expertise extended to breeding and showing poodles, Yorkshire Terriers, and Shihtzus. His success in the field elevated his dogs to the homes of movie stars and company presidents. He later shared this passion with me, teaching me the intricacies of dog shows and involving me in the world of breeding and sales.

The prospect of living together demanded a courageous conversation. We faced the reality that financial constraints would keep us living with our respective parents until we could secure our own apartment. Adding a further wrinkle, Tom's father, Harry, moved back to California and into their house after he and Tom's mother reconciled.

Whenever I visited, I would sequester myself in Tom's bedroom, a space where we shared meals, watched TV, and quietly shared moments of intimacy. Harry's disdain for my presence was palpable, his discomfort evident whenever my car graced their driveway. Despite his disapproval, Antoinette welcomed me with open arms, embracing me as part of her extended family.

A pivotal moment in our relationship unfolded during a

seemingly routine evening at Tom's house. As Tom prepared a plate of food in the kitchen (which was intended for me to eat in sequestration), a heated argument erupted. I strained to listen, and then, to my surprise, Tom's voice rose above the tumult. "I love Les, and I plan to spend the rest of my life with him. Les is going to be a part of this family, or I am walking out right now." At that moment, the trajectory of our relationship changed. I was no longer confined to the bedroom; I was an integral part of Tom's life, officially recognized and acknowledged by him and his family.

Meanwhile, my parents, having met with my counselor, were on a journey of acceptance. They were preparing for a move from my childhood home and had set aside a trousseau of sorts for me — an old toaster oven, pots and pans, kitchen utensils, and some old plates and cutlery.

As time passed, I developed a close bond with Tom's dad, Harry. Despite his initial reservations, Harry grew to love and adore me. We became great pals, and I became his absolute favorite, even surpassing Tom and his sister. On the flip side, my dad formed a deep connection with Tom, to the point where my brother felt a twinge of jealousy at their remarkable relationship. Our mothers, in typical mother-in-law fashion, engaged in friendly competition, vying to outdo each other in supporting us and contributing to our new life together.

The decision to move in together prompted the search for an apartment, an experience that brought to light the overt discrimination prevalent at the time. Rejections from landlords who refused to rent to two men or denied us a one-bedroom apartment were numerous. After a challenging search, we finally found an apartment that welcomed us. On October 2, 1970, we signed the lease, designating it as the date of our commitment to each other and, consequently, the anniversary that would forever mark the beginning of our shared journey. Terrified and excited, we embraced the uncertainty of the future, ready to face whatever challenges lay ahead as we ventured into this new chapter of our lives together.

Moving in marked an unexpected event with its fair share of tumultuous emotions. Tom, in his fear of commitment, staged an argument on our move-in day, storming out and professing reluctance to share a life under one roof. I would later discover that this was a calculated strategy due to his fears of the commitment we were making.

Alone and frightened, I reached out to my father, tears streaming down my face. He told me to give it some time and to be strong. He reassured me that I would be OK either with Tom or alone. Unbeknownst to me, my father's next call was to Tom, a fact Tom would reveal years later.

My father told Tom that there was a remarkable man crying his eyes out and lonely in the apartment he and I were meant to share. My father urged him to reconcile, emphasizing the wonderful life awaiting us in our new apartment. And so, Tom returned, mended the rift, and together, we began our journey as live-in partners.

We were so excited in our first one-bedroom apartment. Though modest, every piece of furniture, every item we had acquired, was a source of pride. A black-and-white TV graced the living room, perched on a TV stand that held memories of quiet evenings together. An old donated couch, used coffee and sofa tables, and a kitchen table from a friend of my aunt's completed our furnishings.

Tom found a used king-sized bed in the newspaper, and we splurged on the cheapest linens and bedspread we could find.

Weekends were our escape, a chance to revel in an authentic and open life, dancing at gay clubs and sharing moments with friends. But Monday brought us back to the challenging and often inauthentic version of ourselves demanded by the outside world. Money was tight, as is often the case in new relationships. No savings, just credit cards, which we used generously, accumulating debt as we steered the complexities of adulthood. We were, after all, still kids.

Even in our early attempts at being grown-ups, love and commitment formed the bedrock of our relationship. However, this didn't spare us from continual bickering about trivial matters.

I often sought solace in complaining to my parents about our squabbles. However, my mother, with a wisdom that surprised me, offered stern advice about the nature of adult relationships.

She admonished me saying, "I don't want to know when you are fighting and I don't want to know when you are making up. If you want to have a relationship, then go home and make it work or end it."

Her words resonated, and I returned home, determined to make it work.

One mature decision we made early on was a pact to never go to bed angry. We promised to resolve conflicts, no matter how long it took. This commitment, made in our early years together, sustained us through the decades. Only once did I break that pact, 28 years later, during an argument that led me to sleep in the guest bedroom.

Tom, true to our commitment, approached me calmly. "We made a commitment 28 years ago that we would never go to bed angry. We are not going to break that commitment now." Tears flowed, and we stayed up until the issue found resolution. Hand in hand, we returned to our bedroom.

We learned the art of compromise, the strength in vulnerability, and the lasting power of love through the highs and lows. Our shared experiences, from our humble beginnings in a small apartment to managing the intricacies of sickness, prejudice, and cultural expectations, established a relationship that went beyond the ordinary.

Our challenges were unique, borne out of being gay, facing discrimination in jobs and careers, and striving to live an open and authentic life. Yet, we were fearless. Best friends, confidants, warriors, and, above all, lovers. Our neighbor, 50 years later, captured it perfectly: "From the first day we met you and Tom, we could see that your love for one another was boundless and everlasting."

Sickness became a different obstacle, one we faced with acceptance, action, love, caregiving, and kindness. The first instance struck at an early age when Tom was diagnosed with prostate cancer at the unusually young age of 49.

Being 45 and 49 years old, facing a life-threatening illness felt like the worst thing that could ever happen to us. Yet, as life unfolded, every time we thought things couldn't get any worse, they did. This pattern would persist through the various challenges we encountered over our 53 years together.

Tom's cancer diagnosis, while frightening, was caught early and his youth played a significant role in his favor. We consulted with a nationally recognized surgeon who recommended a radical prostatectomy, a decision that would impact both our lives profoundly. Armed with a yellow pad full of questions, I sought answers that would guide us through this difficult journey.

The prognosis post-surgery was daunting—2 months of recovery, at least six weeks off work, and the possibility of incontinence for a year or even the rest of his life. We grappled with the potential consequences, ultimately deciding that the loss of continence and sexual prowess was a sacrifice worth making for life. It was a shared decision, a testament to our commitment to each other.

At the time of Tom's surgery, I was the Assistant Superintendent of Instruction in a prominent school district, adding an extra layer of complexity to our situation. At work, I navigated the ordeal without disclosing our challenge, often making excuses to be out of the office and caring for Tom during his recovery. Despite having friends and family, we felt a profound sense of isolation.

To our surprise and relief, Tom's recovery defied expectations. He returned to work in just two weeks, and the incontinence subsided within six weeks. The surgeon, able to perform a nerve-sparing procedure due to an encapsulated cancer and Tom's young age, attributed to the swift recovery. Despite the challenges, we were alive and still deeply in love. We embraced the mantra that we would make it work, and indeed, we did.

As we steered the twists and turns of our extraordinary journey, an unimaginable challenge awaited us—one that would test the very fabric of our love. The road ahead held uncertainties, but together, we were prepared to face whatever came our way. Our story, far from over, continued to unfold, each chapter written with the ink of shared dreams, enduring love, and the unwavering commitment that defined our extraordinary union.

Chapter 4
Confronting Bias, Shaping Success

The road to success unfolded before me, paved with discrimination, disappointments, and challenges that would ultimately lead to noteworthy achievements. Armed with my freshly earned teaching credential in special education, I eagerly embarked on the quest to secure my first teaching position, only to be met with rejection from four school districts. The reasons behind these rejections remained elusive—whether it was my limited experience, my demeanor, or perhaps deficiencies in my interviewing expertise. Faced with mounting discouragement, just as I contemplated giving up, a glimmer of opportunity emerged from an unexpected source.

The chance presented itself in a school district located beyond my familiar territory, in a community in which I had no prior experience. Oxnard High School, was predominantly Hispanic and low-income, with pockets of poverty woven into its fabric. At the age of twenty and a half, I found myself at the precipice of a new chapter, unsure I was ready to face the challenges that lay ahead.

The interview process was swift, with the director of special education recommending my employment to the school's principal for the final nod of approval. The urgency was palpable, as the school year had already commenced, and a vacancy needed immediate filling—a ninth through twelfth-grade classroom awaiting a teacher for 18 educationally mentally retarded students aged 15 through 18. The principal's assessment of me during the interview was cursory at best, but I embraced the opportunity and accepted the position.

Oxnard High School, I would soon discover, had many challenges. A sprawling campus with 2400 students and over 125 teachers, it stood 40 miles away from the middle-to-upper-class community I had known all my life. My first day, a nerve-wracking initiation into this unfamiliar world, began with a disconcerting scene. The school's perimeter was secured by police officers, a sight that hinted at a community in crisis.

As I entered the parking lot, subjected to a security screening, I made my way to the principal's office, only to be greeted by a principal who seemed oblivious to my impending arrival, questioning my very presence and purpose there. The bafflement I felt reflected the uncertainty of the journey that lay ahead, but little did I know that this unassuming beginning would mark the start of a transformative chapter in my professional life.

I introduced myself to the principal, who handed me my teaching contract, a tangible symbol of my entry into the teaching profession, with a modest annual contract of $7200. As I was handed the key to Room 1, I inquired about the school's atmosphere, and he nonchalantly referred to a "little racial issue" that had temporarily shut down the school. The reassurance that everything was back in order did little to quell my rising anxiety. It was a chilling realization that my introduction to this new chapter in my life was to be accompanied by the echoes of recent unrest.

Guided to Room 1, I was met with the expectant gazes of my new students, their faces displaying curiosity and uncertainty. In a bid to assert my presence, I boldly wrote my name on the chalkboard, a small act meant to signify the beginning of a new profession. In my naivety, I sought their perspective on recent events, prompting a candid sharing of their experiences. The underlying tension between "brown kids" and "white kids" had erupted into a student walkout, escalating into physical confrontations that prompted the school's lockdown, police intervention, and a two-day closure. The students recounted these incidents matter-of-factly, painting a vivid picture of the challenges that awaited me.

The school had reopened with a police presence, but the student unrest lingered, a silent undercurrent beneath the surface. This tumultuous introduction to my teaching career was far from what I had anticipated. Towered over by most of my students, navigating language barriers (I spoke no Spanish), and facing young minds shaped by experiences starkly different from my own, I felt the weight of the challenge to establish authority in Room 1. At the age of 20 and a half, I found myself leading a class where some students were just a step away from adulthood. And so, with determination and a touch of trepidation, my teaching career began. Despite my inexperience, I seized control of the situation and embarked on the task of educating my 18 students.

On my first day while returning to my class after a preparation period, I was confronted by a fellow teacher who was on "hall duty." Because the school year had already begun, he not yet been introduced to me. However, I was wearing the mandatory tie and sport coat required of all male teachers.

The teacher asked me "Where is your pass?" Initially embarrassed, I replied," I am a teacher." To which he retorted, "don't give me that smart-ass shit and give me your pass." My response to him was, "I am a teacher, and you shouldn't speak to students that way." I turned and walked away. He and I never spoke to one another for the rest of the school year.

The rapport with my students, initially positive, began to fray as I overheard the whispers, the Spanish slur "maricón" echoing in the corridors. It was a disconcerting realization that my sexual orientation was not only known but also used as a weapon against me. Faced with this derision, I opted for silence, feigning ignorance and choosing not to confront the slur head-on. By ignoring this slur, my students realized for the first time that I did not speak or understand Spanish.

The breaking point came during my third month on the job. In the midst of disciplining a male student and preparing to send him to the office, he lashed out. In a violent surge of anger, he yelled the same slur, "maricón," and delivered a blow to my neck that sent me and my desk skidding across the room. Pain, terror, and shock coursed through me as I grappled with the reality of being physically assaulted for the first time in my life.

Summoning an inner strength I didn't know I possessed, I maintained composure, instructing him to leave the room and report to the office. The other students, frozen witnesses to the altercation, awaited my response. Calmly, I walked into the neighboring classroom, urgently explaining to the teacher the emergency at hand and the need for him to take over. With a heavy heart and a bruised neck, I sought refuge in the principal's office.

There, in a moment of vulnerability, I laid bare the events that had transpired and declared my immediate resignation. The principal, however, urged me to take a step back, go home, compose myself, and take a few days off. He assured me that he would address the situation. I acquiesced, heading home and then to my doctor, seeking relief for what I would later learn was the whiplash I had sustained. Medical professionals recommended pain medications and physical therapy, as well as two weeks at home, marking the beginning of not only healing physically, but also emotionally from the scars of that traumatic incident.

In the aftermath of the assault, I found myself at a crossroads once again, contemplating the path of my teaching career. Fear had taken root, and I grappled with the notion of returning to the same environment that had subjected me to violence. The reality of discrimination, amplified by the slur surreptitiously aimed at me that loomed large, convincing me that acceptance in this realm was unattainable.

Seeking guidance, I turned to my college mentor Barbara Kulik, a seasoned educator whose wisdom I revered and who influenced me to pursue my career in teaching. Her counsel was clear, stern even – I must not succumb to the fear, for quitting would close the door to any future teaching positions. Despite the emotional turmoil and lingering trepidation, I took her advice to heart.

Conjuring up the strength to face my fears, I arranged a meeting with the Director of Special Education and the school principal. They informed me that the student responsible for the assault had been expelled, and the other students were eagerly anticipating my return.

It was a glimmer of support, a small flame in the shadows of uncertainty. Still grappling with doubt, I made the courageous decision to go back.

The faculty room, a space meant for camaraderie and collaboration, became a hushed arena of whispers and sidelong glances. While nothing overt was said, the unspoken tension left me feeling isolated. In a sea of colleagues, I found solace only with one other special education teacher. Despite the challenges, I soldiered on, completing the semester.

As the term drew to a close, I made the difficult decision to resign from the school district. It marked the end of a tumultuous chapter and ignited the pursuit of new opportunities, a fresh start in a profession that I was determined to reclaim on my terms.

The decision to resign from the school district weighed heavily on my shoulders, a culmination of tumultuous experiences and the impact of discrimination. Emotions tangled within me—there was relief, a sense of liberation from a toxic environment that had tested my resilience to the core. However, mixed with relief was disappointment and frustration, a bitter acknowledgment that I had been compelled to abandon a position I had eagerly embraced.

Yet, within the core of this decision, there was a spark of determination—a resolve to reclaim agency over my career, to assert my identity without compromise. The pursuit of new opportunities became not just a pragmatic step but a symbolic act of empowerment.

Leaving behind the echoes of whispered conversations and sidelong glances in the faculty room, I stepped into the unknown, guided by the belief that my skills and passion for teaching should not be overshadowed by prejudice. The decision to resign became an act of defiance, a declaration that I would not be defined by the discriminatory actions of a few.

As I closed the door on that tumultuous phase, I carried with me a mix of emotions—anticipation for the fresh start ahead. It was both a goodbye and a resolute step forward toward professional fulfillment and a commitment to shaping a career on my terms, free from the shackles of discrimination.

After garnering that first teaching job, my teaching career took off with successful positions in both special and general education at both secondary and elementary levels. I was working in a middle- class community, and I was content as a teacher and enjoying my experiences.

To my surprise, I was approached by a school principal who told me she saw that I had leadership ability and asked me to be her 'lead teacher.' She had been assigned by the district to develop a bilingual education program which required her to be off campus on numerous occasions. In the lead teacher position, I still had my classroom responsibilities, but I was to be in charge of the school in her absence to deal with discipline issues and school emergencies.   This would be the beginning of my career in school administration.

Under Susan's mentorship, I discovered a passion for school administration that resonated deeply within me. The allure of leadership and the prospect of shaping educational policies and practices fascinated me. However, as a gay man, my aspirations were tempered by a reluctance to expose myself to the potential scrutiny and biases that might accompany a leadership role in a community interconnected with school affairs.

As I took those initial steps toward a career in school

administration, I was acutely aware that my career path would be laced with challenges. The dichotomy of fear and excitement became a constant companion, and I braced myself for the uncharted waters ahead. Confronting my fears would not only redefine the course of my profession, but also contribute to a larger narrative of inclusion and diversity within the educational landscape.

After 12 years of teaching, and with the pursuit of a master's degree and the acquisition of even more teaching and administrative credentials, the road toward school management proceeded. I began applying for administrative positions, starting with my local school district. Despite my excellent reputation and respect in the region, the doors to administrative positions remained closed, leaving me frustrated and perplexed.

Amidst these setbacks, new mentors entered the scene, bringing with them a fresh perspective and valuable guidance. These mentors played a pivotal role in reshaping my approach and bolstering my confidence. With their encouragement, I broadened my horizons and started exploring opportunities beyond the confines of my familiar district.

As I cast a wider net in my job search, I encountered an unexpected opportunity that beckoned me to venture beyond the comfort of the known. The prospect, though promising, was fraught with uncertainties.

Undeterred by past rejections, I embraced this chance for growth and applied for a district level position in my current school district with resolute determination. The process was arduous, involving interviews, presentations, and evaluations. Each step fueled a mix of anticipation and anxiety as I grappled with the possibility of breaking barriers in my pursuit of a leadership role.

Finally, the moment of validation arrived—an offer for an administrative position. It was not just a professional milestone but a testament to the resilience required to overcome both internal and external barriers. This opportunity would not only mark a significant milestone in my career but also contribute to the broader narrative of representation and inclusivity in educational leadership.

With the unwavering support of Bob Isenberg, my administrative career took a significant turn. Bob was the school principal who initially hired me to be a special education teacher in 1973 where I had begun my career in Simi Valley. Now he was the director of the state and federally funded special projects division at the district level.

Surprisingly, 8 years later, Bob would hire me to be his assistant as his coordinator. I found myself navigating new challenges and excelling in my responsibilities. The recognition that followed was not only a testament to my capabilities but also an affirmation of the impact one's mentor can have on their career.

Bob's influence paved the way for me to work closely with principals, introducing yet another influential figure into my professional career, Shayle, an accomplished elementary school principal with a wealth of administrative experience. Shayle recognized potential beyond my current role and encouraged me to pursue a doctoral degree, setting my sights on the position of a school principal.

The prospect of earning a doctorate was daunting, and I

hesitated, citing concerns about time and financial constraints. However, Shayle's response was a resounding call to action: "You will never have more time or money in your life; get off your ass and get it!" Encouraged by his words, I embraced the challenge and committed myself to the pursuit of a doctoral degree.

Shayle's mentorship continued beyond mere encouragement. He became an integral part of my doctoral dissertation committee, providing guidance and support as I navigated the rigorous process. I did not know then that Shayle's role in my life would extend far beyond academia.

Shayle's guidance and mentorship became a cornerstone of my academic career as I dug into the nuances of my dissertation. His advice not only pushed me to finish my dissertation, but it would eventually play a vital role in unanticipated elements of my life, changing the path of my personal and professional story in ways I had yet to discover.

During my tenure as a district level coordinator, one ordinary day, Fred, one of 16 school principals in the school district, stuck his head into my office.

He abruptly said, "How do you feel about corporal punishment?" I was dumbfounded and replied, "I don't believe in it."

To which he replied, "Well, we are not going to get along very well."

I had no idea what this was about. I went to Bob and shared with him the exchange that I had just had with Fred. Bob then informed me that I was going to be transferred to Fred's school as his assistant principal. Fred was not someone I would ever want to work with.

The abrupt revelation about my impending transfer to Fred's school as an assistant principal left me stunned. The unexpected encounter with Fred, inquiring about my stance on corporal punishment, served as an ominous prelude to a significant shift in my career. Seeking clarity, I turned to Bob, hoping for some insight into this sudden turn of events.

Bob explained that the decision stemmed from the need for my expertise in handling special education programs, as the school Fred oversaw housed such programs. Despite my reservations and the stark misalignment of principles between Fred and me, I learned that I had no say in this matter. The prospect of working under someone with such a fundamentally different approach to education was daunting, and I couldn't shake the sense of apprehension that accompanied this new chapter.

The transition from a coordinator's role to that of an assistant principal brought forth a wave of challenges. Fred's outlook, particularly on disciplinary measures, was at odds with my own, setting the stage for potential conflicts. However, I was determined to steer this professional shift with resilience and a commitment to the well-being of the students under my purview.

As I stepped into the role of assistant principal at Fred's school, I found myself grappling not only with the intricacies of school administration but also with the interpersonal dynamics that played a crucial role in shaping the educational environment. This experience would become a test to my personal and professional growth, presenting unforeseen opportunities for self-discovery and resilience.

Despite the challenges and the palpable discord working alongside Fred, my determination to escape this unfavorable situation only intensified.

After two years with Fred, I recognized that I needed to extricate myself from this stifling environment. I embarked on a relentless pursuit of principalships in neighboring school districts. However, success eluded me, and the reasons behind the repeated rejections gradually became evident. It was a period of reckoning, a time when the harsh reality of discrimination and bias came sharply into focus.

Amidst this struggle, a glimmer of hope emerged when I became a finalist for a principalship position in a neighboring school district. The positive feedback and encouraging signals from the interviews fueled my optimism. The anticipation of a breakthrough, however, soon transformed into disillusionment.

During this critical juncture, a surprising call from my former boss and mentor, Bob, added a new layer of complexity to my predicament. His unexpected request for an informal meeting over a beer at my house raised questions and piqued my curiosity. As I awaited his visit, I did not know that this encounter would hold the key to unlocking the mysteries surrounding my thwarted career advancements.

As Bob delicately shared the clandestine details of the neighboring district's superintendent's call, a wave of conflicting emotions surged within me. My sexual orientation was questioned by the superintendent, although Bob would not confirm that, and it had become a barrier to my appointment. This was not only disheartening but also ignited a torrent of anger, sadness, and a profound sense of injustice. The weight of the discriminatory decision left me feeling defeated and deflated.

Bob's discomfort during this difficult conversation reflected my own, emphasizing the gravity of the situation. The superintendent's admission, veiled in prejudice, painted a stark picture of the obstacles I faced solely because of my identity. The knowledge that my skills and qualifications weren't in question only intensified the injustice of the situation.

Later on, I found out that Bob spoke with Shayle about the matter. Shayle, who supported me and served as a mentor during my career, advised Bob to speak with me about the matter at hand.

Shayle persisted in supporting me and assisting me in navigating the confusing array of possible options. He didn't publicly support LGBTQ+ people, yet he still stood by me and wouldn't let me give up. He never stopped telling me to be myself and be happy with who I was, and to keep looking for administrative jobs. He was certain that I would get the chance to be evaluated only on my abilities and expertise.

The internal debate echoed the broader societal challenges faced by LGBTQ+ individuals in the professional sphere. As I grappled with this profound setback, the decision to persist or reassess my career path hung in the balance, poised to shape my professional journey.

The frustration and anger that welled up within me during this tumultuous revelation became the catalyst for a profound reassessment of my career. The discriminatory barrier that my sexual orientation had prevented me from advancing into school administration, forced me to confront challenging questions about the path I was on.

The contemplation began with a fundamental query: Was school administration truly the right fit for me? The harsh reality of discrimination posed a daunting obstacle, casting a shadow over the aspirations I had held for leadership roles within the education system. The prospect of continually facing prejudice and bias raised concerns about the toll it would take on my well-being and professional fulfillment.

The internal struggle led me to grapple with a deeper dilemma: Was I prepared to endure persistent discrimination for the sake of a career in administration? The idea of navigating a professional landscape tainted by bias begged the question of whether the potential rewards of leadership were worth the emotional and mental toll.

The revelation served as a pivotal moment for introspection, prompting me to consider an alternative path—one that aligned with the core joys that drew me to education in the first place. The classroom, with its intimate connection to students, the daily joys of teaching, and the profound satisfaction derived from witnessing student success, emerged as a sanctuary from the discriminatory challenges of the administrative realm.

The consideration of giving up on the dream of advancing into administration became a palpable contemplation. Was this setback a sign that my true calling was within the classroom, where the impact on students' lives felt more immediate and gratifying? Perhaps the struggle against discrimination would be better waged within the confines of my chosen vocation, where the focus could remain on fostering growth and learning.

The decision at this juncture held the weight of self-discovery and a commitment to a career path that not only showcased my abilities but also provided a nurturing environment for personal and professional satisfaction. As I wrestled with these questions, I stood at a crossroads, poised to define my vocation based on a profound understanding of my aspirations, identity, and the realities of the world I inhabited.

The period of profound reflection led me to a resolute decision—I was worth the fight. Recognizing my talents, expertise, and the potential for meaningful impact, I resolved to continue down the path I had chosen. The obstacles and discriminatory barriers that loomed before me became challenges to be faced head-on, not deterrents to my aspirations. It was an assertion that I, as an individual, deserved the opportunity to be seen beyond preconceived notions.

Embracing the possibility of effecting change, I entertained the idea that as people began to see the person behind the label, they might also recognize the talents and abilities I brought to the table. The notion wasn't driven by grandiosity or conceit but by a genuine belief that visibility and authenticity could pave the way for acceptance and understanding. Perhaps, in my journey, I could become a role model, making a meaningful difference for those facing similar struggles or those who would come after me.

With determination to fight against discrimination, I faced the professional arena with renewed vigor. The rejection from the other school district served as a temporary setback, but the resilience within me prevailed. After several unsuccessful applications in my own school district, the unexpected principalship in the very school where my teaching career began in Simi Valley, was a turning point that defied conventional expectations.

As I went through the quiet hallways of Simi Elementary, the reality of the revelation hit me—it was all mine. The once-impossible post of principal had become a practical reality. I tackled the challenges that were ahead with a great feeling of purpose, prepared and armed with confidence.

The support and affection that emanated from the school community enveloped me. Staff, students, and parents alike extended their warmth, creating an atmosphere that transcended the ordinary. The halls echoed with more than just the sounds of footsteps; they resonated with the shared commitment to learning, growth, and acceptance.

The environment felt like heaven—a shelter where authenticity and dedication were not only acknowledged but celebrated. The dream of success, once confined to the realms of imagination, had now materialized into a tangible, fulfilling reality. The journey, fraught with rejection, discrimination, and moments of self-doubt, had not only led to personal triumph but also became a testament to the power of resilience and authenticity.

Every challenge met, every obstacle overcome, and every act of genuine self-expression contributed to carving out this path to success. It was a realization that one's authentic self, when embraced and presented to the world, could inspire change, foster understanding, and, in this case, lead to the realization of professional aspirations.

From rejection to triumph, the narrative had shifted from being defined by societal expectations and discriminatory barriers to one of personal agency and accomplishment. It was a story of not just breaking through barriers but dismantling them, paving the way for others who might face similar struggles. My new position now stood as a testament to the resilience of an individual who dared to be true to themselves, even when the world seemed resistant to acceptance.

As the end of my first year as a principal was coming to an end, I was attending a dinner recognizing outstanding administrators in our county. It was at this gathering that my life would take yet another turn which would propel my career, but not without challenges and discrimination.

Shayle, once again, proved to be a supportive ally. He was at the event and wanted to speak to me. I remember clearly him taking me outside for a short walk. He put his arms around my shoulders and said, "Les, I have an opportunity for you that will change your life forever." He told me about a notice for the position for a Director of Curriculum and Instruction that was perfect for me.

Despite my reluctance, I decided to seize the opportunity and apply for the position in the South Pasadena Unified School District. It was a role that seemed tailor made for my diverse skill set and extensive experience. As I submitted my application, I viewed it as more of a learning experience in interviewing for district-level administrative positions rather than a serous bid for a career change.

The prospect of driving 60 miles to a new position, coupled with my deep satisfaction as a school principal and the joy I found in my current career, initially deterred me. I had waited a long time to achieve my dream of becoming a school principal, and I was not eager to uproot the stability I had finally attained. I conveyed these sentiments to Shayle, emphasizing my lack of interest in relocation or a lengthy commute.

Shayle, however, saw beyond my reservations. He reminded me that he wasn't guaranteeing the job but encouraged me to view the application process as a valuable experience. It was an opportunity to hone my capability in interviewing for future higher administrative roles and explore potential career paths where I could leverage my diverse experiences and training.

With Shayle's words in mind, I entered the application process with a sense of both curiosity and detachedness. This seemingly innocuous undertaking would turn out to be a watershed point in my professional experience, opening doors to unexpected opportunities and challenges that would transform my career path. The choice to apply, spurred on by a mentor's support, marked the start of a new chapter—one that would put my talents, resilience, and potential for growth to the test.

The interview process was a wonderful experience. I was very comfortable with all of the written exercises and the first of what would be three interviews. I was feeling fairly confident and was not surprised to be asked back for each subsequent interview.

The anticipation that followed the second interview was palpable. Lou, the superintendent, had left a positive impression, and I felt a genuine connection during our conversation. His fatherly demeanor created an atmosphere of comfort, and it seemed we shared a mutual understanding of the role I could play in his leadership team. As we delved into the details of my professional journey—from my initial teaching position to my current role as a principal—we explored the nuances of my specialized training and even touched upon the research I undertook for my Master's and Doctorate degrees.

Lou concluded our meeting by providing insights into the school district and its community. Established in the 1880s, the district boasted a rich history and was an integral part of the community, characterized by a blend of affluent and working-class families. The words he spoke painted a vivid picture of a place with a strong identity and a sense of pride. The district, in essence, was the community.

The final interview loomed as a decisive moment. Lou had indicated that I was one of two candidates being considered, and the suspense intensified as I awaited the outcome. The prospect of joining a leadership team dedicated to shaping the education landscape in such a storied community fueled my desire to succeed. The culmination of this interview process would not only determine my professional future but also present unforeseen challenges and opportunities that would shape the next phase of my career. The exercise that began as a learning experience had evolved into a pivotal juncture, with the potential to redefine my role and impact in the field of education.

The prospect of meeting with the Board of Education stirred a mix of excitement and nervousness. The board, composed of five accomplished and opinionated women, represented the final hurdle in the interview process. Their strength and education credentials were apparent, creating an environment both daunting and exhilarating. However, the interview turned out to be a positive experience, marked by engaging conversations that allowed me to showcase my qualifications and vision.

Despite the promising encounter, silence ensued in the weeks that followed. Concerns about the lack of communication prompted me to reach out to Shayle, albeit with reservations about taking advantage of his wife's role as the superintendent's secretary. This decision unveiled unforeseen challenges.

Shayle conveyed disheartening news—although I was the selected candidate, a majority of the board faced difficulty reaching a consensus to hire me. The stumbling block? A couple of the board members harbored concerns about my sexual orientation, fearing potential issues within the community. Learning about this prejudice left me devastated and angered. I declared to Shayle, "I am done. I am withdrawing my application. I have worked too damn hard in my career to be recognized for my achievements and not for the person I love, and I will not do this anymore!"

Expressing my frustration, I asserted my intention to remain in my current school, where I felt valued and respected as a principal. Shayle, in his attempt to provide solace, urged me not to give up. He emphasized that quitting now would allow them to judge me solely based on who I loved rather than considering my expertise and accomplishments. His words served as a rallying cry for authenticity and conviction, urging me to stand firm and be unapologetically Les. The decision to continue the fight, guided by principles and personal integrity, laid the foundation for the next stage in my professional journey.

The internal struggle of whether to embrace the challenge or retreat to the familiar continued to torment me. I struggled with disappointment, anger, and fear, yearning for the comfort of the known. Why should I willingly step into a situation where acceptance might be lacking? What additional hurdles would I encounter if offered the position? Moreover, the decision not to relocate added another layer of complexity.

A few days later, a call from Lou added a new twist to the narrative. He affirmed that I was his preferred choice but disclosed the need to secure support from a couple of board members. In response, I explained my imminent trip to Alaska, rendering me unavailable for the next few weeks. However, Lou suggested an immediate meeting over lunch in the district, catching me off guard. Despite my reservations, I agreed to the meeting.

During our lunch conversation at the local coffee shop, Lou, unaware that I was privy to the controversy surrounding my candidacy, expressed enthusiasm about having someone of my caliber on his team. As he extended an offer that placed me on the highest step on the salary schedule due to my experience and advanced degrees, I was left dumbfounded. Lou attempted to convince me to join the district, shedding light on the contentious dynamics among the five women board members who, despite their differences, he believed could be rallied to support my appointment.

In a moment that surprised even me, I found the courage to assert, "I have a wonderful job now in a community that appreciates me and respects me. I would not be able to leave my current position unless there is a unanimous 5-0 favorable vote of the Board to appoint me." This declaration, rooted in a commitment to my current community and a demand for unequivocal support, set the stage for an unexpected turn in the unfolding saga.

Lou responded, "I will try my best to get a 5-0, but this school board rarely unanimously agrees on anything."

As Tom and I started on our much-anticipated trip to Alaska, the weight of questions pushed down on me, each with the ability to change our lives. What if my nomination was unanimously accepted by the board? Would I be willing to quit my current position, relocate our lives, and face the hardships of a fresh start? How would I handle interactions with my present employees, and what was the genuine nature of the route I was considering? The internal fight persisted, and I couldn't help but feel a mixture of worry and resentment— half jokingly directed at Shayle for forcing me into this perilous path.

While exploring the magnificent landscapes of Alaska, the dramatic scenery outside reflected the tumult within. Tom and I shared the awe of glaciers and the enchantment of a pristine wilderness, but my mind kept circling back to the impending decision that awaited me. The trip, designed for relaxation and adventure, became a backdrop to a personal saga that unfolded in the corridors of my thoughts.

In Anchorage, the days blended with the spectacular views of glaciers and the hum of uncertainty. When the agreed upon time came, I made the call to Lou as planned. The phone call, sharing the outcome of his meeting with the school board hung in the balance. I remember depositing the numerous quarters into the payphone and while doing so, my heart raced.

As I listened to Lou's voice, I could sense the weight of the decision he was about to share. The finality of his words would shape the direction of my career and, consequently, my life.

The payphone echoed with the surreal news. Lou had achieved what seemed both improbable and daunting—a unanimous 5-0 vote by the board, a resounding endorsement of my capabilities and a validation of who I was. Lou's ecstatic voice, declaring his success, reverberated through the receiver, and the weight of that moment settled upon me. There was no turning back; the course of my life had taken an unexpected turn, and I was on the brink of a new chapter.

Lou's triumphant announcement left me momentarily speechless. The acknowledgment that I had secured the position I hesitated to embrace, was met with a mix of emotions. There was a surge of pride and a sense of accomplishment for overcoming the hurdles posed by discrimination. Yet, an undercurrent of trepidation persisted this leap into the unknown held both the promise of greatness and the specter of challenges yet to be faced.

Before I could even express my acceptance, Lou had already initiated the employment process, reaching out to my current boss and laying the groundwork for my transition to South Pasadena. The Alaskan wilderness, which had served as a backdrop to my inner conflict, now unfolded outside the payphone booth, a stark contrast to the tumult within.

The majesty of glaciers and the rough terrain of Alaska acted as a strange background to my churning thoughts as the cruise progressed. The beauty of the environment clashed with the unknown of the way ahead, leaving me torn between the pulls of exhilaration and worry. The remaining days of my vacation and the return trip home were now tinged with the poignant realization that life, in all its uncertainty, had given me a chance that required both bravery and perseverance.

After one year, my position as a Director of Curriculum and Instruction was advanced to Assistant Superintendent, which meant I would be second in charge of the school district. After Lou's retirement two years later, I was appointed to succeed him as superintendent where I would remain for 12 years before being recruited to lead a school district in Northern California. Success!

Chapter 5
From Turmoil To Triumph

My objectives have always been connected with the dream of becoming an educator. I can go all the way back to when I was ten years old and set up my imaginary classroom in my garage. One wall had a chalkboard, a present from my wise father. As a young teacher, I would be there teaching classes to a group of imaginary students that were only in my head. Even if the specifics of those early classes have since faded, I can still hear the excitement I felt as I projected lessons and shared knowledge.

My childhood fantasies and my growing enthusiasm for education met in this modest garage, which was turned into a classroom. I had no idea at the time that my early role-playing would eventually solidify into a lifetime dedication to molding young minds and encouraging a love of study. That chalkboard, a silent chronicler of the early phases of my academic adventure, marked the start of a path that, year by year, would provide me with fulfillment and purpose.

The idea of an imaginary classroom in my garage provided comfort and empowerment during the difficult early stages of my education, which was a sharp contrast to the anxieties I experienced in the real world throughout elementary and middle school. Those early educational years were filled with the echo of childhood insecurities that resounded down every street, intensifying the internal struggle that took place against the backdrop of my vulnerable self-esteem.

Instead of being a source of identity, the name "Leslie," which was a distinctive identifier, created a constant state of fear. Every day seemed to be a war zone where my name was used as a weapon and a constant reminder that I was different from everyone else. "That's a girl's name" was a recurring mockery that resonated deeply, accompanying me everywhere I went in academic hallways.

A horrific companion on this journey, bullies, added another complication to my already intricate connection with schooling. My anxiety would also peak on test days or the dreaded "vaccination day," when I would do anything to avoid having to get vaccinated since I was afraid of needles. I even tried to manipulate the thermometer in my desperation to make it look like I was sick, but my mother's sharp eye would usually see through the act.

Nevertheless, I was able to escape the harsh reality of the campus by disappearing into the safety of my house. My imaginary classroom turned into a sanctuary where I could enjoy being a teacher to my imaginary students. I had no idea that this early retreat into fantasy would set the stage for a day when the terrifying hallways of my early years would no longer exist. I got mired in the difficulties of being a student who found it onerous to succeed in the regular school environment as I made my way through the challenging terrain of my academic path.

Despite all of this disorder, three people stood out for their kindness: Mrs. Peel, Miss Orson, and Mr. Smith. Their compassion and warmth offered moments of relief from the otherwise difficult voyage. These early elementary school teachers spotted promise hidden within me, even if they had difficulties figuring out my learning style. Their faith in the undiscovered potential within me was an indication of hope in the gloomy pathways of my schooling.

The struggle continued, and the traditional method of instruction frequently left me lost in academia, looking for a lifeline. I was desperate for direction and for someone to acknowledge my special aptitude for learning. Without customized help, I was left to struggle with the challenges of being a student who felt like a square peg in a round hole.

My memories of those early years are marked with a need for understanding and a painful longing for someone to help me navigate the intricate web of schooling. I had no idea that this difficult trip would ultimately lead to a profound revelation of my ability for progress and that these lessons would finally result in true learning.

I was aware that during my elementary school years, my family was struggling financially. I was determined to take some action to relieve their burden so I became a kind of entrepreneur and found jobs at my school.

Every morning I began my job of filling the school's refrigerator with the day's delivery of the supply of milk. I also volunteered for a variety of duties during lunch hour, such as helping with lunch trays or washing dishes, and that became yet another venue for my sincere efforts. The remuneration for my work was a free lunch every day, which was a wonderful reward for my labor. The free lunches relieved my parents of part of their financial burden and spared my mother the trouble of making my lunch every day.

In addition to the evident benefits, the free meal provided me protection from the harsh realities of lunchtime bullying, which frequently lingered on the playground. During such times, the school cafeteria served as a refuge, a place where the hardships of our financial circumstances were temporarily overcome by the comfort of a shared meal and an escape from my classmates' cruelties. I would use these early lessons in resourcefulness and perseverance as a foundation to help me continue to negotiate the complexities of life's problems.

My elementary school routine came to an abrupt stop when Mr. Smith, the person in charge of the volunteer jobs, decided it was time for someone else to take advantage of the opportunity I had grown to value. I was completely taken aback by the news. It was like receiving an electrical shock. I lost my job and I was no longer responsible for those everyday tasks. It also took away a free meal, which was intended to ease my parents' financial burden. But this would not thwart my efforts to continue my entrepreneurial aspirations.

A crucial point in my early life was when I moved from elementary school to the intimidating world of middle school. The upcoming arrival of puberty contributed additional levels of stress to an already hostile environment. Getting through middle school meant figuring out the elaborate locker system, interpreting the seemingly mysterious combination lock, and facing the difficult task of switching between different classrooms with six different teachers during each of the six class periods.

But the true test was still to come in the field of physical education, which is full of puberty-related difficulties. A deep sensation of terror overcame me at the thought of getting dressed and, even more unsettling, showering with my teenage classmates. Many accepted these rites of passage with a casual ease, but for me, they amplified the fears that had long been my constant companions. The shift to middle school was like traveling across unknown waters, with self-doubt rebounding louder than before.

The scary thought of moving to middle school was somewhat eased by my brother. He was a kind guide who took me to the school one summer day to get acquainted with the complex layout of the buildings and the maze of lockers as my first semester approached. He provided priceless insights into the intricacies of managing relationships with different teachers. In the meantime, my mother, who knew I would have difficulties in physical education, went with me to the neighborhood sporting goods store to get the necessary t- shirts, shorts, and gym shoes.

Even with these attempts to make my shift easier, the anxiety's weight showed up in bodily illnesses. In my adolescent years, I experienced irritable bowel syndrome and even had an ulcer. The anxiety of the unknown, combined with the constant threat of bullying, permanently altered my middle school experience.

Even now, I can't quite figure out how I got through those turbulent years. Perhaps it is an act of disassociation to conceal some terrible memories. The sounds of bullying, the physical threats one endures for the enjoyment of others, and the uncomfortable feeling of being pushed through crowded halls remain eerie recollections of the difficulties that characterized those early years.

The chorus and theater group provided me with a sanctuary in the middle of the difficulties I faced. It was a place where I could feel comfortable and accepted.

My passion for performing created an interest in me, and I made friends with others who had similar hobbies. In addition, I discovered that I found myself drawn to the school band and decided I wanted to play the clarinet. As a sign of their dedication to fostering my interests, my parents paid for private lessons to help me pursue my enthusiasm for playing a musical instrument. They went so far as to give up money to get me my very own clarinet, which was a really meaningful gift to me. Even though I wasn't a particularly good clarinetist, the instrument allowed me to enter the world of the school band, which gave me a feeling of purpose and belonging during those unstable years.

The experiences I had in high school were varied and full of both positive and negative aspects. An important source of comfort was a job experience program that provided a way for me to graduate from high school early. Even though I participated in the drama club, concert and marching bands, the academic side of things was still difficult for me.

Being in the marching band turned out to be a blessing because our rehearsal sessions coincided with the physical education period. I was spared the agonizing experience of having to attend the tense regular PE classes. However, the educational problems continued, with geometry and algebra standing out as particularly puzzling courses.

Even if high school may not have completely removed the obstacles I continued to face, these extracurricular activities gave me moments of comfort and companionship in the midst of the challenges of the classroom.

I discovered a way out of the abyss by switching to general education instead of college prep. This choice allowed me to graduate from high school early and eased the graduation criteria. In spite of school, I had a busy social life outside of school.

I took part in a lot of social activities, going to parties, dancing, and even courting girls. Unexpectedly, I started going to proms and was invited to go on multiple dates. These social interactions gave me happy and supportive moments and a much-needed break from the challenges I had to overcome in my academic career.

I got engaged to Sandy, a lovely girl, when I was nineteen. But after roughly nine months, our engagement ended. Astute and direct, Sandy said that I wasn't quite there and didn't give her the love connection she had hoped for. Her choice was actually a relief in hindsight because it gave me the opportunity to explore my own identity and goals freely. It signaled a sea change in my life and set me on the path to and development.

Many years later, Sandy and I happened to run into each other in the grocery store. We hugged, and she pulled a shopping cart with two children. She proudly revealed her story and that she had become a teacher of the deaf and hard of hearing. During that brief encounter, I told her that after several years of my own teaching, I entered school administration and earned my doctorate.

Naturally, curiosity provoked inquiries about our personal lives. I answered Sandy's question regarding my marital status by saying that I was single. Sandy smiled politely, sensing the subtle nuances, and said, "Your parents must be so proud of your accomplishments." We left with the unstated knowledge that our decisions had put us on different but rewarding paths.

Throughout high school and college, I devoted a large amount of my time to employment. I was able to support myself by working at a medical laboratory operated by my father's friend. This experience opened the doors to taking on several jobs in other medical labs as well. This financial security also gave me the opportunity to buy my first car when I was sixteen years old. During my undergraduate years, living at home further reduced my financial burden and increased my personal savings.

While academics remained a priority, my passion for performing arts took center stage. I was invited to join a band as the lead vocalist called The Five Young Men, performing at weddings, bar mitzvahs, and similar events. The allure of acting also captivated me, and with unwavering determination, I decided to pursue a career in the arts. Taking it seriously, I invested in professional composite photos, sought out an agent, and even adopted a stage name—Les Anthany, spelling it differently to stand out. With the means at my disposal, I engaged a vocal coach to refine my talent and propel my artistic ambitions forward.

My pursuit of a career in the arts turned out to be a short-lived endeavor. Despite securing an agent who facilitated numerous "open call" auditions, success eluded me. I showcased my singing talents at open mic nights and a few intimate club gigs. While I landed a couple of commercial jobs, the requirement to join the union and pay dues significantly diminished my earnings, leaving me with only a meager income.

Deep down, I grappled with the realization that my aspirations for a life of financial comfort and luxury were not aligning with the unpredictable life of an artistic career. It was a tough acknowledgment that prompted me to reassess my professional path and consider more stable alternatives.

An impactful conversation with my talent agent marked a turning point in my artistic ambitions. With a sense of sincerity, he emphasized the all-encompassing dedication required for a successful career in performing. He conveyed the need to prioritize this path above all else, embracing the challenges of rejection and the uncertainty of a financially precarious lifestyle. However, reflecting on my aspirations and values, I realized I wasn't prepared to make the necessary sacrifices.

At that moment, I made the poignant decision to bid farewell to Les Anthany and close the chapter on my pursuit of a singing and acting career. It was a sobering acknowledgment that paved the way for a new direction—one that would ultimately shape my journey and lead me toward a more grounded and sustainable future.

The transition to college was nothing short of transformative for me. It became a place where I discovered the joy of being a student and ignited a genuine passion for education as a lifelong pursuit. My initial struggles with poor grades and SAT scores were overshadowed by the nurturing environment of the community college I attended.

In this setting, the professors understood the unique needs of their students and went above and beyond to provide the extra attention necessary for success. What struck me most was the presence of classes dedicated to essential study skills—how to study, take notes, and write papers. It was a revelation, a resource that I sorely missed throughout my earlier educational journey, particularly in high school.

College, for me, became more than an academic pursuit; it was a passion. While I hadn't yet defined a clear direction for my future, the atmosphere of learning, exploration, and camaraderie among likeminded individuals created a sense of purpose and belonging that I hadn't experienced before.

In college, my motivations became more pronounced, and one in particular loomed over me—the military draft. To secure a student exemption, I needed to carry a minimum of 15 units and maintain a C average. However, my ambitious decision to enroll in 18 units during my first year at Valley College was met with skepticism. The entrance counselors, basing their judgment on my high school performance, entrance exams, and SAT scores, insisted that it was too much for me.

I took the challenge head-on, unaffected. I had to file an appeal against the decision, arguing persuasively to the dean's office why I ought to be permitted to take on this tough course load. I saw this as my profession, and if I failed, I alone would suffer the consequences. That was my argument, plain and simple. Maybe convinced by my perseverance, the dean agreed to let me take 18 units.

What followed was a remarkable achievement. Not only did I manage to carry the heavy academic load successfully, but I also earned a place on the dean's list in my first year—a testament to my tenacity. All this while juggling a demanding work schedule, dedicating twenty to thirty hours a week to employment. It was a challenging yet fulfilling period of my life.

Transitioning from a two-year college to a four-year institution was a monumental step for me, a move that promised expanded horizons and greater academic challenges. My commitment to education and my proven academic competence opened doors to a myriad of possibilities. However, the reality of my financial limitations and the desire to remain close to home influenced my decision to enroll in a local college.

The choice to stay in my familiar surroundings, even as I pursued higher education, was both a practical and emotional one. Limited financial resources compelled me to make pragmatic decisions, yet the familiarity of home provided a comforting anchor amidst the academic whirlwind. As I embarked on this new chapter, I carried with me a blend of excitement for the academic opportunities that awaited and a sense of groundedness in the familiar landscapes of home.

Amongst the scores of academic possibilities, I found myself standing at the crossroads of choice when it came to selecting a major. After much contemplation, I settled on speech communications, a field that seemed to resonate with the multifaceted aspects of my personality. With a passion for performing and a desire to explore the diverse realms within the communication sphere, I believed this choice would pave the way for many career opportunities.

As I delved into my major, the academic journey unfolded with captivating courses and thought-provoking professors who not only expanded my knowledge but also enriched my perspective. Alongside the academic pursuits, my circle of friends grew, forming bonds that were not only significant but imbued with love and understanding.

During the course of my studies, fate seemed to intervene when I stumbled upon an elective course during my first year – "Introduction to Teaching Special Needs Children." I had no idea that this elective would become a pivotal moment, steering me towards a path that would shape not just my academic journey but the course of my entire life.

Barbara Kulik, the beacon of influence that she was, emerged from the pages of my academic journey as one of the most impactful figures in my life. Engaging in her course, I was captivated by her warm and compelling teaching style. Our conversations, born out of shared enthusiasm for the subject, took unexpected turns, ultimately leading Barbara to encourage me to consider a career in teaching, specifically with special needs students.

The decision to embark on the path of education was met with disbelief from my parents. Given the challenges I faced as a student, they couldn't fathom why I would willingly choose teaching as my profession. In response, I shared a piece of my heart with them, explaining that it was precisely because of my challenging student experience that I felt compelled to become the kind of teacher who could make a profound difference in a child's life.

I wanted to be a mentor for children who were going through similar things. Teaching, with all of its difficulties and victories, became my life's purpose. It was a calling that spoke to me deeply and developed into a passionate relationship. Every minute spent in the classroom was treasured and full of a deep sense of fulfillment that comes from being in the field of education. I loved relationships with the kids, the curriculum's complicated demands, the parents' collaborative attitude, and my colleagues' togetherness.

I realized that teaching not only helped me to share my knowledge with others but it additionally empowered me to have a significant influence on the development of young minds. It was a life-altering event that will never fade from my memory and profoundly improved my life in ways I never could have predicted. I had found contentment and happiness in the classroom, which had formerly caused me fear and insecurity while I was a student. Here, I flourished, and in turn, I assisted others in growing. I had conquered.

Chapter 6
Home Is Where the Heart Is

The early days, months, and years put Tom's and my relationship to the test since, despite our families' calming presence, the outside world remained unfriendly to anyone who dared to love differently. We faced apartment rejections in our search for a home; every door that was banged shut reflected the larger rejection from a society that failed to acknowledge us. However, in the midst of hardship, we finally secured a small one-bedroom apartment that served as both a home and a symbol of our enduring love.

We cultivated a home furnished with reused furniture that spoke of tenacity, a colorless TV that depicted our surroundings simply, and a modest choice of plates and cooking utensils that facilitated our meals together. Despite their lack of extravagance, each object carried our pride and served as a reminder of our resolve to build a future together. We took comfort in those walls, protected from the sounds of public contempt, turning an ordinary room into a sanctuary where our love grew unaffected by the challenges outside.

Initially, there was no artwork on the walls. Later, however, we carefully hung art prints, and the once-bare walls became a gallery of our shared memories.

We frequently felt the burden of financial distress as we weathered this difficult time. Tom's choice to give up dog breeding created a gap in our finances, and I had to take on the role of main provider with my low salary. The apartment rent, utilities, and car payments, were all harsh financial realities that needed to be carefully considered. Despite the difficulties, the love that grew behind the walls of our small apartment and our shared devotion served as the motivation to get us through those turbulent early years.

In his way, Tom struggled with motivation when confronted with the reality of our circumstances. In a vulnerable moment, I made a final request for a balance in our shared responsibilities. I was afraid of being alone, but I had no choice but to take the chance. I told Tom that he had to find a job or move out! The ultimatum miraculously worked.

Tom got a job at BelAir Travel, one of the most prestigious travel agencies in Los Angeles. Though it was entry-level employment, it worked as a lifeline to stability. Even with his small salary, his help relieved the financial burden. Weekends became enjoyable times when we could just breathe and be with each other after our week long commutes to work.

After living together for only nine months and following the incident at Oxnard High School, and my subsequent resignation, I began the search for new employment which proved to be more difficult than I had imagined. I had applied for numerous teaching positions but was rejected every time. Why did it happen all the time? I had stellar recommendations and sound experience. Could it have been that I "presented" as gay?

I was panicking with the fear of potential unemployment. I considered crazy business ideas like selling Herbal Life or Shaklee goods because I was so desperate to make ends meet. But in the middle of all of this chaos, a glimmer of light appeared in my way, and I was hired to teach primary special education pupils at a private school.

The sad truth of the low pay for the role, however, tempered the relief of getting a job. However, in the bigger picture of things, this work turned out to be a lifesaver, something that gave me perspective and shelter.

The private institution's complex workings were made clear by its unique dynamics. California Law required a strict ratio of credentialed and non credentialed teachers at the school. They actually needed me to meet this requirement and so I filled a position as the only fully qualified teacher in my grade range, which included grades 4-6. Despite possessing the necessary state certification, my career path unexpectedly split when I was subordinated to a senior colleague who did not possess the same qualifications. This contradictory situation served as an important reminder of the sacrifices one must make in order to maintain a career and, eventually, a means of subsistence.

That year seemed like it would never end, with every minute carrying the burden of unhappiness and hopelessness. The school was owned by a heartless proprietor motivated only by greed rather than fostering the development of young minds. I was disgusted by the owner's cruel dismissal of pupils who paid less tuition in order to make a place for more profitable opportunities.

The toxicity spilled over into the relationships between my fellow educators and went beyond the classroom. I was treated like an inexperienced person in a situation where people who ought to have been my supporters disregarded my experience and knowledge, all in an insecure setting. The sense of community that defines teaching as a career fell apart, leaving me dissatisfied and disillusioned.

Tom had an adventurous spirit that went far beyond just seeing new places; it included searching relentlessly for a house that could adapt to our shifting objectives. Even with few means, we were driven to seize opportunities despite what seemed to be insurmountable challenges because we had a deep-seated yearning to establish a home of our own.

Our persistent search for a place to call home continued to be arduous. Our combined dynamic power of Tom's unyielding energy and my unfailing dedication carried us onward. Every apartment rejection we faced and every obstacle we overcame strengthened our determination to find the right place. And every rejection we experienced made us more determined to establish a life where we could flourish in spite of all the odds against us.

Our search brought us, in an expected course of incidents, to the front door of a home with a surprising promise. The agent made an emotional pitch as we considered renting, and he presented an array of possibilities including purchasing. I shared with him that I was seeking a teaching position and that once I was able to secure one, we would be in a better position to consider owning.

The universe surprised me with kindness. Motivated by friendliness and goodwill, and probably the potential to make a sale, the real estate agent put me in touch with his friend – who was the assistant superintendent of the local school district. This led to the unexpectedly quick and easy realization of an opportunity. The assistant superintendent called me and I was hired to teach summer school at an elementary school. This position was given to me without the traditional interview or formality practices. It was evidence of the quirks of fate, a lucky meeting that would turn out to be a key turning point in our search for a home of our own.

With the summer school opportunity serving as a potential conduit toward a permanent position, I was determined to make a name for myself in the district. My hopes were raised by the summer school principal's affirmations, which came in the shape of wonderful recommendations. A door opened, moving my application for a teaching position into the "approved candidate pool," where my potential would be exposed and my worth assessed.

My future became more accessible, and as fate would have it, I was to teach at Simi Elementary. A new chapter in my professional path began with the challenge and satisfaction of mentoring learning disabled kids in grades 4-6. This journey would not only define me professionally but also serve as a living example of the tenacity of a desire born out of pure determination and constant enthusiasm.

We did decide to move to a new apartment, even though the idea of owning a house remained unattainable. This decision was a conscious attempt to put us closer to the domains of our professional lives rather than just a simple change of address.

Driven by his wanderlust, Tom created travel options that fit through the tight spots on my teaching schedule. However, even if these experiences were abundant, there was a price paid that was intangible. The allure of deals drew us in, and with each one, we edged closer to financial stress and further from home ownership.

Tom, the eternal optimist, strongly argued that youth and energy were ephemeral and pushed us to enjoy the present, even at the expense of mounting debt.

Our passports turned into memory pages, marked with the luxury of five-star hotels, flying first class and experiencing trips that opened up new vistas for us to explore. These changes were made possible by Tom's connections in the elite travel industry, as suppliers begged his company to include their services in the itineraries of his travel agency clients. We may have incurred debt, but we had a treasure trove of experiences that, looking back with no regrets, taught us about life and living, exposed us to different people and cultures, and gave us immeasurable enjoyment and happiness.

Tom's boss, and the owner of BelAir Travel had a strong affection for me. She included me in many business get-togethers and meals. I saw a real affection in her eyes, an understanding that went beyond the work environment. I thanked my wealthy aunt silently for her etiquette training, as we made our way through the country club activities, making sure that I could handle the world of cutlery, which is an unseen language at these parties.

My association changed from that of an observer to that of an active participant as I referred potential customers to Tom and BelAir Travel. Mrs. M. became aware of my referrals, and suggested that I try my hand at outside sales for the agency. During the summer break from school, I became a relentless door-knocker and cold caller, bringing in significant income to the agency and enhancing my own income with earning commissions.

But even in the excess of discovery, a mild caution ruled. Our travel plans were meticulously planned and executed; there was never a request for a king-sized bed, and there were periods of hiding in the lobby while Tom checked in. Leslie's persona occasionally provided a barrier to presumed heterosexuality. So as long as I remained invisible we were daring enough to secure that king sized bed!

As the sun set on this chapter of BelAir Travel, Tom's reputation as the travel agent's travel agent par excellence soared. He started pursuing employment closer to home. It seemed like the right move to accept a position at a new agency that was only a few minutes away from our home. Two years later, our migratory impulses returned. Change was the only constant for us. Ever the restless soul, Tom looked out to new horizons, pondering the next trip, move or new experience to enrich our lives together.

While exploring a new residence to rent, the Universe was smiling on us once again. The real estate agent was also the owner of the house.

She asked, "Why rent when you can own?"

Aware of our financial situation, I jokingly responded with, "Because we have no money!"

She then retorted with, "That's OK. I have another property. I can make this arrangement work for you." The world in its mysterious ways, demonstrated once more that kindness could sometimes appear as a kind stranger.

The decision to become a homeowner was an act of faith motivated by the trusting innocence that frequently accompanies aspirations. The residence was a townhouse that was only a short distance from our comfortable apartment. The house seemed perfect, and everything came together when the realtor—a kind agent of fate—unveiled a scheme driven by the owner's complicated "double escrows" and a common desire for fresh starts.

In this peculiar financial balancing act, our journey to become homeowners took on the unusual. A $10,000 loan from Tom's father was deposited in our bank account to make an appearance that we had the required amount of funds to qualify for the mortgage. A 90% loan application and a calculated showing of the money in our savings were the cryptic steps that led to the escrow closing. When escrow closed, the $10,000 was redirected into Tom's father's account. We found ourselves not just as residents but also as homeowners as a result of the creativity and help of others who wanted the best for us.

The first excitement of owning a home was soon replaced by the reality carved into the walls of our new abode. A new set of challenges appeared when the previous residents moved out and what was left in their absence. The walls reflected the faint traces of their tobacco smoke, tracing the outline of the headboard that had formerly occupied the main bedroom with pride. The quiet of the dishwasher represented our financial limitations, and the lack of a washer and dryer dimmed our hopes for a complete home.

Our parents came together in the face of these challenges and helped us by putting together enough money to paint the inside of the house. Our house was far from perfect nor did it represent what we had envisioned in our minds, but we were proud homeowners and proud of this milestone.

Our exploration of the complexities of shared ownership led to legal issues. To protect our investment and one another, every transaction we entered into required that it be executed into a joint ownership agreement. The insurance complexity followed, negotiating life insurance, taxes, and careful will drafting entwined with joint tenancy. We accepted the awkward and unfamiliar legalese with frustration, anger, and sadness that we were to be treated differently because we were unmarried men.

Another truth emerged in the field of medical emergencies: our parents and siblings controlled our destiny. Because we were not married, the hospital's doors might be banged shut during irregular visiting hours, as those were reserved for families only. If Tom or I needed surgery, we feared the surgeon or nursing staff could keep important information from one of us, the perceived outsider.

Our vulnerability resulted from our reliance on family relations as well as the lack of legal recognition. Amidst a maze of possible dangers, trust emerged as a crucial element. Without formal relationships or marriage, protecting our common assets became a grave responsibility, and we hung onto the hope that our relatives would not take advantage of any weaknesses resulting from our nontraditional situation.

Our anxieties were shadowed by the catastrophe that befell our closest friends, Bob and Jerry. Bob's brain tumor brought an end to a ten year partnership and left Jerry helpless against medical bureaucracy.

Unpredictable visiting hours were reserved for the family, Jerry was unable to get information or answers from the surgeon. This injustice, highlighted the significant influence that social approval and legal acknowledgment might have on the lives of individuals who dared to love beyond social norms.

The terrifying aftereffects of Jerry and Bob's tragedy continued to ring in our minds, serving as a sobering reminder of the dangers associated with unacknowledged connections. Bob's death shadowed Jerry's independence. After emergency brain surgery, Bob's family took over without him ever being conscious. A moving time of closure, the funeral ceremonies turned into a battlefield where Jerry's voice was silenced, and the hierarchy of the family won out. Jerry was excluded from the service and had to stand on the periphery of his sorrow.

As if the loss of a spouse wasn't enough pain, Jerry also became entangled in a ghastly web of kinship avarice. A portion of the house's revenues was requested by Bob's opportunistic and alienated family, who selectively chose items from their shared life. Jerry's complaints were ignored and overshadowed by threats of publicity and legal disputes. Jerry gave in to the terrifying demand, robbing him of the last vestiges of a life united.

Sitting in horror, Tom and I felt both heavy with empathy and relieved at the same time that our families were close by, united by our common ideals of love and respect. But beneath the surface, a question hung like a spirit: would our families respect and defend us and our union?

The intelligent and observant members of our families knew the true nature of our relationship. There were questions in the air, unsaid but clearly felt about our relationship. Tom's mother, brushed questions off with the straightforward instruction to "ask them." My mother accepted the reality, blatantly proud of and proclaiming our partnership.

We visited our respective families in Chicago frequently. We were Tom and Les; no need for excuses or explanations. Our extended families accepted us for who we were and allowed our years together to erase any sense of difference, exemplifying the beauty of unconditional love.

But like any story, there were disagreements at times. An invitation to my cousin's wedding carried the pain of rejection. My cousin, three months my junior, was getting married. Larry and I were inseparable until college when he went off to the east coast. Written exclusively to me, the wedding invitation glaringly ignored the fact that Tom and I were partners, and only I was invited. I was hurt beyond words. It was a painful reminder that discrimination persists even in the most accepting environments.

My decision not to attend the wedding, threatened to tear apart the very foundation of family relationships. I mustered up the bravery to call my parents and tell them how Tom and I were in a relationship and there was no way I could go to my cousin's wedding without him. They were horrified that I would not attend. Because we were a close knit family how would they explain my absence? Their fear of being judged, clouded their reaction. They insisted that going to the wedding was a debt owed and reminded me of their love and support.

Nevertheless, I remained firm. However, my father gave me a devastating ultimatum that severed the relationship between us. My father who had been my closest ally did not support me. During that heated conversation, I refused to accept my father's conditional approval and held fast to the idea of unconditional love. With a sorrowful heart but a strong spirit, I muttered, "I thought you loved me unconditionally. I still love you and I will miss you." For the sake of love and truthfulness, I broke a parental tie, declared my love, and faced an uncertain future with those words. After that exchange, he and I stopped talking to one another.

In the middle of the broken relationships and unsolved disputes, my mother's call signaled the start of another tense conversation. The weight of social expectations was reinforced when she insisted that I call my cousin and explain my decision to Larry. We didn't say much to one other, and the discussion concluded with an implicit admission of the widening gap.

I called Larry and informed him that I would not be able to attend his wedding without Tom. I told him that whether or not he approved of my relationship with Tom, we were a couple married or not.

Larry claimed that the impersonal "numbers" were the reason Tom wasn't invited. I couldn't let go, though, without voicing the unfairness of our connection. "The 'numbers' would work if either Tom or I were a woman or if we were married," I said, addressing the underlying prejudice that was present. He asked me to at least attend the ceremony without addressing the unspoken facts. I simply ended the call telling him that I wished him the best.

I called my father's bluff anyway, not letting weakness win out in favor of love and self-assertion. As Tom and I set out on a planned 21 day journey across South America, our usual airport farewells gave way to a bus transfer to the airport without the usual well- wishes and bon voyage kisses and hugs from my mom and dad.

When we got back to the States, there was a moment of truth. Anticipating a lonely trip home, we were surprised to see my parents waiting outside the customs area, which was both beautiful and comforting. We avoided the difficult subjects that had caused splits between us during that silent reunion in favor of warm hugs and stories about our travels.

As Tom and I entered our house, we saw that the refrigerator had been stocked with food, as well as an array of new plants in our home representing a silent pledge of acceptance and reinforcing the enduring power of familial relationships.

I spent over ten years apart from my mother's family as a result of that turbulent stand. The absence of my uncle, aunt, and cousins caused a gaping hole that obscured the semblance of my relationship with my mother's side of the family. My aunt and uncle had been my mentors and their absence served as a sobering reminder of the abyss that our alienation had caused.

Their influence went beyond the material gifts they gave me. My aunt was not just a giver of money; she also became a curator of life's finer points, introducing me to them all. From sumptuous meals to thrilling theatrical productions, from mesmerizing music to profound artistic expressions, they bestowed upon me an education that extended beyond the confines of textbooks—a curriculum intertwined with affection, appreciation, and the common delight of discovery. Their terrible absence created a hole that time was unable to fill, demonstrating the lasting influence they had on the story of my life.

I reflected on her annual buying of my fall clothes for the next school year when I was in elementary school. It was a kind and nurturing gesture. Her son, my cousin Larry, and I were the same size, so she could buy two of everything. These actions were more than just financial support; they were symbols of love and compassion.

In the middle of my father's many and unfortunate illnesses, the hospital accidentally served as a setting for healing my family relationship as well. I followed a rule of decency, even with those strained ties, giving a soft peck on the cheek and a courteous acknowledgment during those hospital visits when my aunt and uncle were present. Perhaps detecting a small win in my ability to keep my composure, my mother expressed her delight in my ability to uphold the familial link in spite of the underlying tension. It was a gesture that served as evidence of a code of conduct that was ingrained in me from my upbringing.

As the years passed, ten years after our extended breakup, Tom and I were given a real olive branch in the form of an invitation to my aunt and uncle's fortieth-anniversary celebration, which was specifically directed to us both. The invitation was in the form of a poem and printed in green ink on a linen card. I accepted the invitation writing back to my hosts in a poem and also in green ink on a linen card. This conversation, a word exchange in poetry, served as a conduit for our communication that went beyond spoken words, which had been absent from our lives for years. Recognizing the nuances of this symbolic encounter, my aunt expressed to my mother her excitement and respect for the "class" I had demonstrated—an unspoken bridge mended through the language of ink and verse.

Tom and I attended the event, which was held at my aunt and uncle's home in the posh neighborhood of Holmby Hills, not far from the famous Playboy Mansion. As we made our way to the grand entryway, the valet took care of our car. A guest book, complete with a picture of every visitor on a blank page, was waiting at the door, an exquisite touch for writing heartfelt wishes to the happy couple. A page in the book with a picture of Tom and me together made our incredulity change to awe, a testament to the tacit acceptance and acknowledgment from a family that had previously ignored us.

Once through the doorway, there was one more pleasant surprise in store. My uncle greeted us with sincere kindness. When Tom thanked him for being included, my uncle's reaction was amazing. My uncle replied, "No, thank you for coming," and placed a gentle kiss on Tom's forehead signaling his acceptance in a way that was deeper than any words of consolation. The same love was shown to me, and in an instant, no words were necessary to dissolve the last vestiges of distance. The quiet hug spoke volumes, and in that private instant, the distance that had followed us for years vanished.

After the walls of silence were broken, Thomas and Leslie set out on a life that spanned 53 years—a remarkable adventure filled with prosperous jobs, homes in both Northern and Southern California, and travels across the world. But behind the calm surface of our story lay an uprising that would eventually shatter my very being.

Chapter 7
Threads of Love, Strands of Loss

Tom's mother was diagnosed with Alzheimer's disease in the 1990's. I saw in 2013 that Tom was exhibiting some of the same traits. He frequently lost his sense of direction, struggled with everyday household chores, and was atypically confused about our location.

I told our primary care physician about my concern and indicated I was extremely worried about it. I was communicating with her in writing, so as not to let Tom know about sharing my concerns with her. Because of Tom's respect for Dr. Sarayba, I thought that he would comply with her directives. However, after speaking with Tom during a routine office visit, she was not persuaded that he needed assistance.

Two important events occurred soon after that visit, which is why I again insisted that Tom be evaluated. The first was when I watched him in the kitchen getting ready to prepare a lasagna, which was something he could do in his sleep and had done a million times. Tom had all the ingredients arranged as I stepped into the kitchen. Tom was just staring at the empty lasagne pan.

"What are you doing?" I inquired.

"I don't remember how to do this," was his response.

His voice carried worry and disappointment. I intervened right away, starting to assist him and demonstrate what he had consistently done.

The event, however, that altered our lives most significantly was when Tom got into a vehicle accident. Tom was deeply upset by the accident, which was obviously his responsibility. He never drove again because he developed a driving phobia. He said he was concerned about driving since the accident had scared him so much. In hindsight, this was a godsend as I never had to forbid him from driving or seize his vehicle. Our doctor agreed that Tom needed to be assessed when I told her about these experiences.

We scheduled the neuropsychologist's appointment. The fact that we would be receiving some conclusive information was extremely important to me. However, Tom declined to attend the appointment a few days prior. I wrote to Dr. Sarayba once again since I was very upset by his refusal to go. This time, she informed me that she believed Tom might push back if we insisted he see the specialist. However, one year later, as the decline of Tom's cognitive abilities became more apparent, Dr. Sarayba was able to convince Tom to see the neuropsychologist, and this time, Tom relented and agreed to go.

When we arrived at Dr. Horne's office, she indicated that the evaluation would take two hours. She asked me to leave and return after she had sufficient time to conduct the extensive testing.

I was desperate to pass the two hours of anticipation by keeping myself occupied. I returned to the waiting area after the two hours and Tom was still seated at the doctor's desk. The door to her office was open. Tom looked back at me as I sat in the waiting room.

"I failed," he murmured as he turned to face me. I was heartbroken.

Dr. Horne then invited me to enter her office at that point. "You did not fail, but it is evident that you had some difficulty completing many of the tasks," she stated to Tom.

She wanted to know if we wanted her to review the testing with us right then and there, or if we would rather wait and talk to Dr. Sarayba about her findings. I informed her that I would want to review her results at that time because this was her area of expertise. Tom concurred.

She shared examples from the test to demonstrate areas where Tom was cognitively impaired.

"Whatever we name it isn't important," she continued. "Tom clearly was suffering from a neurological condition that would cause emotional and cognitive capacities to deteriorate further."

She suggested that we visit a neurologist for additional assessment. Tom didn't seem to understand what she was saying, even though I did. I had a glimpse of what was ahead because I had previously gone through this with Tom's mother.

My heart was heaving with emotion as I drove home from the appointment. Tom stated he didn't want to talk about the appointment.

It took several months to get an appointment to see a neurologist to review Dr. Horne's diagnosis of Tom and to advise us on the next steps.

We saw Dr. Young, a well-respected neurologist in the Coachella Valley specializing in Alzheimer's and Parkinson's Diseases. Dr. Young was wonderful. He was kind and gentle and respected our marriage and relationship. He included me in all the conversations and constantly asked me how I was and what I was doing to take care of myself.

After his review of Dr. Horne's findings and his own physical tests, he was straightforward in stating that Tom did have Alzheimer's. He ordered an MRI to find out how severe the disease was on his brain to help decide on a path forward.

Two weeks later we had that fateful follow-up appointment with Dr. Young. In his forthright but kind demeanor, he had us focus on his computer screen which held the image of Tom's brain. He pointed to the x-ray showing us where the plaque buildup was, and pointed out the significant amount of brain tissue that was damaged.

He informed us that the disease had caused irreversible damage to Tom's brain.

Tom did not react, I'm not even sure he comprehended what he was being told. I was trying not to faint, throw up, or cry. He told us to continue to live our lives as best we could and that we would deal with each phase of the disease as they arose. He advised me to get support for myself and to be prepared to become a caregiver.

I can't express how terrified I was after that appointment. I heard what I knew the outcome would be, but now it was real. I was devastated. I was now completely in charge of both of our lives. I was now completely responsible for everything. I felt alone and afraid.

My life entirely changed after Tom's diagnosis in March of 2020. He would now need my constant attention and care 24/7. This was significantly complicated by the COVID pandemic and the impacts that this crisis had on all of us. I can't even imagine how I would have navigated this time of my life had I not been retired. My new full- time job was that of full-time caregiver.

I saw over the period of five years as Tom's condition steadily declined, the tragic deterioration into the worst stages of Alzheimer's. His identity and ability to think gradually worsened. The steady decline of cognitive abilities was demonstrated by the way what started out as normal memory loss turned into a maze of anxieties and perplexity. As time went on, I observed Tom's independence fading and his capacity to comprehend the world around him reducing, along with his deteriorating mental abilities.

After a great deal of research done secretly in my bedroom walk-in closet, I engaged a caregiver who would come for three hours twice a week to attend to Tom and to give me some time for a respite. This was no easy feat, as Tom did not want to have a caregiver, but he capitulated when I lied that I was not well, and I was going to the doctor. As he did not like being alone, I convinced him that it was important for me to have someone with him in my absence so I would not be worrying about him.

After interviewing with a home care provider, Carol would be assigned to care for Tom. She was a lovely woman who had a great deal of personal experience with dementia patients. She told me she would provide activities for Tom like coloring, working on puzzles, and baking cookies. But Tom would have none of that. He didn't like it when I left, and Carol was unable to engage him in any activities. He watched some television but spent most of the 3 hours standing at the front door waiting for me to return.

During the few months that followed, Tom continued the decline. He could no longer read or write. He was in a constant state of confusion and needed continuous attention.

One day I came home after a short break when Carol asked me to walk her to her car. She told me that she was concerned about Tom and me and that I should consider placing Tom in a memory care facility. She said out loud what I had been thinking in my head but was too afraid to acknowledge.

During the next couple of weeks when Carol was with Tom, I explored potential places for Tom's full-time care.

As I visited the various locations, I was running on pure adrenaline. After I conducted the visitations, I settled on an assisted living home that had a secured memory care unit which housed 25 residents with dementia.

I signed the contracts, completed the voluminous paperwork, and Tom would be moving into his new home in two weeks. I immediately went to a furniture store and purchased a dresser, two nightstands, two matching lamps, an electric recliner chair, and a small kitchen table and chairs. These would be delivered to the apartment in a few days. Next, I went to a mattress store to buy a bed and bedframe followed by stopping at an appliance store to purchase a television. I then bought all the linens and necessary toiletries which I hid in the backseat and trunk of my car for a future delivery.

During the following days, I removed several wall paintings from our home to hang on the walls of Tom's new apartment. I took framed photographs of Tom and me to place on the nightstand and dresser. I surreptitiously and carefully placed the necessary clothing in his new closet and dresser when I had access to the apartment to set up before Tom moved in. When the furniture arrived, I made the bed with the new crisp matching linens and set up his bathroom.

The days leading up to moving him into his new home at Atria were filled with fear and overwhelming sadness. When the moving day was upon us, I used a strategy I learned from my training by the Alzheimer's Association.

I would tell a "therapeutic lie" to get Tom into his new home. I told Tom that I was having a "procedure" and that I would be in the hospital for a week or so. I said that I could not leave him alone while I recuperated, so I found a place where he could live for a short time. He never asked what the "procedure" was or how long I would be gone. Nor did he ask me where he would be living.

My emotional angst and pain when leaving him at Atria that fateful day, will forever be etched in my mind. Tormented by the disease and the loss of the love of my life was indescribable.

I returned to our house without Tom for the first time and sobbed uncontrollably. I looked on the wall at my favorite photo of us during our last trip to Maui and looked at the two of us and spoke outloud, "I am so sorry to do this to you. I love you and miss you."

Tom's placement at Atria did not ease his persistent issues or my emotional strain. Even after moving into a care facility, the responsibility for handling the complex nature of Alzheimer's illness continued. I went to see him every day, planning my visit to arrive at 10:00 so that it would coincide with his lunch at 11:00.

During my visits, I tried to involve him in different activities offered by the institution, but he persistently refused to take part.

Instead of making use of the services, he showed a liking for alone time, spending much of his time in his apartment's chair watching TV. Even though there was a nice patio outside that was good for hanging out in nice weather, he was more likely to get back inside his apartment as soon as possible after spending little time outside.

Each time I visited for the next couple of months it was pure torture when it was time to leave. As I walked toward the elevator to leave he would say "please take me home" or "how could you do this to me." And each time my heart was broken into pieces yet again.

Once he was finally comfortable and appeared to accept his new living arrangements, I scheduled trips to take place at least once a week. These outings usually consisted of lunch dates at familiar restaurants, barber appointments, and sporadic trips to the nail salon for pedicures and manicures. These excursions were enjoyable for him, and fortunately, he always consented to going back to his apartment without any major problems.

The stability of these arrangements was challenged after an event in which he fell and became unable to walk. He thus had to adapt to permanently living in a wheelchair.

After 13 months, Atria began to feel like an "institution" rather than a home. I sought out a better placement.

I had heard of board and care homes that accepted Alzheimer's patients. The idea of Tom being in a home rather than an institution was compelling. Most of the board and care facilities are limited to 5 or 6 residents and have at least two caregivers on duty at all times. It was time to make a change.

At AM/PM, Tom experienced a higher degree of individualized care within a family home atmosphere. The home was conveniently located a short 4 miles from our home.

While Tom received attentive care, my own path toward solace and acceptance stretched dauntingly ahead. The quest for inner tranquility and the resumption of personal life activities demanded profound resilience and introspection.

Weekly counseling sessions and regular attendance at Alzheimer's support group meetings provided essential avenues for emotional processing and community support. Despite these efforts, pervasive sadness, profound loneliness, and debilitating depression persisted unabated.

It seemed unsettlingly different from the usual to be alone in our home. All of my life had been characterized by living with someone else, from my parents' house until that day in 1970 when Tom and I set up our first apartment. My recent isolation had left me struggling with a deep sense of insecurity and a lack of experience adjusting to such a solitary way of life.

Trying to figure out what to do with my time when I wasn't visiting Tom, proved to be a difficult task. I had no interest in cooking and no desire to entertain myself other than watching TV in the evenings, so I was at a loss for what to do. The previous five years had been entirely devoted to Tom's care, and his new placement created a gap that made every day feel uncertain.

The advice to start taking antidepressants was followed after consulting with my counselor. In order to treat my ongoing insomnia, my doctor also recommended medicine that induced sleep at the same time. Unfortunately, these measures were unable to reduce my feeling of hopelessness, and despite the use of medicine, sound sleep was still elusive and limited to a few hours each night.

Even with the resolute assistance of sympathetic friends, accepting invitations to social functions and get-togethers was another challenge. I was so uncomfortable being the only single person in a room full of couples that I was unable to participate completely in these events because I was only thinking about missing Tom.

In addition to my counseling and support group, I became a voracious reader of books on living with Alzheimer's and dementia, death and dying, and grieving.

These did not help me; instead, I became even more depressed. I truly cannot remember how I was functioning. But somehow, I just kept putting one foot in front of the other and moving along as best I could.

Chapter 8
Final Days with Tom

Tom's severe deterioration continued shortly after he moved into his new AM/PM residence. He was now under hospice care, with regular visits from the hospice workers. His degeneration was both mental and physical. He lost interest in everything. He spent days sitting in his wheelchair at the kitchen table. He didn't want to watch TV or look at the photographs in the travel magazines I brought him. He sat still, staring at his surroundings.

Seeing him slipping away right in front of me was frightening. I tried to stay strong for him, but it was tough. Every day was a battle against despair. It was hard to watch him lose interest in everything he used to love. We used to talk for hours, but now he just sat there, lost in his own world. I felt like I had lost him already, even though he was still there. Hospice workers came and went, but they couldn't ease the ache in my chest. I tried to keep myself busy, but there was a constant weight on my shoulders. I missed the days when we could laugh together when there was still light in his eyes. But now all I could do was hold his hand and hope he knew how much I loved him.

His conversation was confined to yes/no questions. But his eyes lit up the moment I stepped into the room, and I was always greeted with a wide smile that revealed his charming dimples. He'd even acknowledge me with the pet names he'd given me during our relationship. The staff would comfort me that he recognized me and knew who I was, even at the end of his life.

Tom dropped over 100 pounds from his 5'10" body in the

months leading up to his death, down from 260 to 130 pounds. His bones protruded from his body, and he developed bed sores due to the lack of skin between his body and his torso. He had transformed into a skeleton, yet he could still chew and swallow food, and his organs were functional. His eyes would open, and he'd react to my words and touch. His death was approaching in the final month of his life. His organs were beginning to fail, and death was nigh.

Throughout this dreadful time, Tom continued to respond to outside stimuli, but his response became more rare. He would occasionally open his eyes and respond to physical and auditory stimuli. He would react most strongly to human interaction and the soothing sound of familiar voices. But as his final months progressed, the signs of his approaching death grew increasingly obvious.

While I took a managerial position to plan and manage logistics, I was also emotionally tight as I braced myself for the impending loss. I had to accept the truth that Tom was going to die soon, and that meant I had to be strong enough to bear the responsibilities that arose.

Tom and I were ahead of the curve, organizing pre-need funeral services together in 2010 to prevent some of the logistical hassles of end of life arrangements. All it would take to carry out our planned approach was a phone call to the designated mortuary. The primary element of the plan was cremation in accordance with his wishes, followed by placing his ashes in the niche we had carefully picked together. He had specified that he wanted no fuss, no formal funeral or commemoration. I would, however, keep some of his ashes to scatter in Maui, our favorite vacation destination.

In the final week of Tom's life, Dr. Surgarman from hospice was brought to his bedside after Maria, the hospice nurse, indicated the need for a doctor's examination. After reading Tom's medical records and having a cursory glance at him, the doctor turned to face me. In a calm tone, he delivered his professional judgment, anticipating that Tom would not survive much longer. The caretakers were advised to discontinue all food and oral medications, and the nursing team began administering morphine every four hours, which is a routine palliative therapy implemented when a patient's death is imminent. And so started the dramatic finale of Tom's journey, the beginning of his final path.

During Tom's last days, I kept a constant watch at his bedside with occasional visits by Russell, the AM/PM administrator, and Maria, the hospice nurse. When Tom's life was coming to an end, Maria and Russell, recognizing how crucial this time was, asked whether I wanted to be with him when he died. Families with similar circumstances routinely seek this.

Thinking back on our 53 years together, I informed Maria and Russell that Tom and I had finished our trip through life together. Our shared experiences, warm comments, and conversations encapsulated the essence of our union. As a consequence, there were no unresolved issues between us or unspoken words. The most essential thing I wanted to say to Tom in his final hours was to reassure him that both he and I would be OK.

I felt Tom was in pain in his final days. When I voiced my anxiety, Maria tried to soothe me by explaining that Tom's state was typical of the dying process. She emphasized that the morphine was administered to alleviate Tom's agony and suffering. However, witnessing Tom's physique degrade, despite her assurances, did little to alleviate my fears.

I was sitting by his bedside the Monday afternoon before he died. I lied my head on his bed while I stroked him gently. He was making odd noises, which made me much more anxious than before. I contacted Mary Lou, the respected facilitator of our Alzheimer's support group, a close confidante with much understanding of death and dying, and a good friend. I explained my worries to her and sought her expert assistance.

Mary Lou told me that what I was witnessing was the natural course of the dying process, which is rarely observed firsthand. She responded kindly, realizing how distraught I was, and advised that I contact the hospice nurse again to discuss possibly increasing Tom's morphine dosage.

I summoned Maria, and she returned to Tom's bedside. She confirmed what Mary Lou had told me about the act of dying. After checking him, she informed me that Tom showed no symptoms of distress, but she would prescribe medicine to help him relax. She also doubled his morphine dose every two hours.

Maria shared with me a concept based on her considerable experience dealing with death and dying: our loved ones typically wait until we are not around before dying. There are numerous family members leaving their terminally ill loved one's hospital room only for them to die while they are gone. She stated we should all believe what we need to believe, but Tom may be waiting to be alone before passing away.

I waited until sunset to say my final farewells. However

witnessing Tom's body degrade did little to alleviate my fears. I knew in my heart that I wouldn't see him again. I told Tom one last time how much I loved and valued him for bringing me so much happiness.

I kissed his forehead and said, "It's fine, let go. We'll both be OK."

Buoyed by adrenaline and power I had no idea I possessed, I made my way home for the night.

Following a challenging night, I awoke early the next morning as I prepared for the day's necessities, which included a small selection of food and drink (granola bars, water), as well as some books and an iPad for reading and distraction.

I yelled out a somber statement that echoed throughout my silent house, "I don't think I can handle this for another day."

At 7 a.m., I received the predicted call from Russell notifying me that Tom had died between 3 and 5 a.m.

I knew that his death would bring an end to his anguish and suffering, liberating him from the constraints of disease. Furthermore, I imagined that his death would relieve me of the arduous task of seeing his gradual decline and collapse. But the fact that he was physically missing brought a whole other dimension of grief. The inability to simply touch him or kiss his forehead or run a hand through his hair, triggered this unhappiness feeling the void that had been left behind.

Watching Tom deteriorate over time was terrible. Witnessing him battle the same affliction as his mother for a decade was like enduring a never-ending hurricane. It was uncanny that both Tom and his mother battled this same disease for 10 years and they both died at the same age of 78. It felt like history repeating itself in the cruelest way.

Each day was a struggle to maintain composure, to be strong for him and for myself. But beneath the surface, I was wrestling with a myriad of emotions – fear, sadness, and an overwhelming sense of helplessness. It was a turbulent time, and the toll it took on me was more profound than I dared to admit.

Chapter 9
Looking for Peace in the Present

I had an epiphany several months prior to Tom's passing that altered my life and provided me with a means of adjusting to my new situation. My friends Steve and Jovino expressed their worry for me and my depression as we were eating lunch together one afternoon. They told me about a Japanese philosophy that they believed I should consider adopting since it had a beneficial influence on their lives.

Ichigo Ichie is a multi-translated Japanese adage that has its origins in a Zen Buddhist principle. Its meaning is "an opportunity in this moment." In order to live Ichigo Ichie, one must look for significance in each moment. Ichigo Ichie advises us to let go of anxieties, melancholy, fury, and other unfavorable feelings by making use of the five senses.

I bought "The Book of Ichigo Ichie" after taking their advice to heart. I started studying and using this ideology after finishing the book and doing some of my own research. I worked diligently to pay attention to my surroundings, savoring the sounds, sights, and fragrances while realizing that each moment is fleeting. Being present requires not just being aware of the positive things around us, but also admitting to and attempting to let go of any bad feelings.

Including Ichigo Ichie in my life has had a very positive impact. I now see every moment through the lens of this Japanese philosophy, which has evolved from a simple guiding principle that helps me discover value in even the most mundane parts of life. My leg is permanently marked with a tattoo of the Japanese characters for Ichigo Ichie, which acts as a continual reminder to embrace life to the fullest and enjoy every moment, no matter what obstacles I face.

Despite being inundated with self-help books about loss and death, one book that my kind friend Nita sent me spoke to me deeply. I was struck by Megan Devine's book "It's OK That You're Not OK," which is full with insight. There were two ideas in particular that really stuck out throughout the text.

The first concept is that of getting "under" grief rather than getting "over" it. This has allowed me to acknowledge and accept the pain of loss as a part of my journey. The grief of our loved one will always be with us. But if we put it under us, allowing the grief to sit on the foundation of our being, then we can begin to build a new life on top of it.

The second concept is moving "forward" as opposed to moving "on." It would seem semantic to distinguish between moving on and moving forward. However, moving on implies forgetting about someone or something and leaving them behind. On the other hand, moving forward requires us to start a new beginning without ignoring the past. This small change in viewpoint has given me the confidence to take a fresh approach and embrace new options.

It used to seem impossible for me to find pleasure and joy after Tom passed away. However, I started to get past my sadness and live in the now, opening my heart and mind to the opportunities that were all around me.

I will carry Tom with me everywhere I go because he will

always be a part of me. Bereavement never goes away; it only takes on different shapes. I started going out again, taking part in social events, and even accepted the notion of traveling again as part of the healing process.

Being resilient in the face of life's many challenges is a difficult task. I was successful in life because I had a loving upbringing and was inspired to take on all of life's obstacles. I overcame discrimination by making an effort to be true to who I am and by asking to be valued and acknowledged for my individuality and character. I achieved professional success by pure willpower, going above and beyond to fulfill my life's ambitions. I took advantage of every chance I was given and overcame all obstacles along the road, even hardships. Most crucial, though, was that I succeeded in love.

My existence and affection serve as a tribute to the courageous men and women who came before me. Tom and I were able to go forward on the path toward acceptance, achievement, and love because of their hardships. My goal is that my story will inspire those who are currently struggling with similar issues today. Or possibly give one a "me too" moment when they can identify and perhaps feel they are not alone in their struggle. Every person has a unique narrative to tell, we can all benefit from each other's experiences.

I am 75 years old and on the verge of a new chapter in my life. I am not just existing, I am actively living. My constant friend, mindfulness, helps me face every day with hope and resolve. My experience has gained a significant depth by interacting with the Alzheimer's Association, which has enabled me to return the favor to a community that has supported me both before and after Tom's sickness.

I am dedicated to having a positive influence through my participation in the Alzheimer's Association community education, fundraising, and the creation of an LTBGQ+ support group. These initiatives seek to overcome social and legal barriers in order to solve the specific issues that my community faces. In the same way that the Alzheimer's Association helped me and gave me resources, I now try to be a source of understanding and strength for others.

I cling to the hope that one day, in President Biden's words, memories of Tom will "elicit smiles rather than tears." My 53 years of combined experiences and beautiful recollections form a vibrant tapestry with shifting patterns and sequences. Even though every moment is different, they all fit together beautifully to form our shared life.

Today, I reflect on my life with Tom with thankfulness and contentment. I am resolved to let go of anger and fear, to live in the present and treasure the memories of a life well-lived, and I will keep viewing every event as an opportunity.

I can still relate to my mother's wise advice to my 12-year-old self. "Your life ahead will be filled with many bumps in the road and unexpected twists and turns, but you, my dear, will surmount them all and be a successful man." And Leslie did; and is!

About the Author

Leslie Adelson, M.A., Ed. D. retired after a 39-year career in education, business, and consulting. Dr. Adelson received his Masters Degree from Redlands University in Special Education and his Doctorate from The University of LaVerne in Organizational Development. He held various positions including teacher, school principal, and Superintendent of Schools. He was an adjunct faculty member at California State University Northridge, Santa Clara University, and UCLA. He has been a speaker at numerous conferences and has provided coaching to upper-level school administrators, school boards, and business leaders. He is published in a number of educational journals, and his work has been recognized and cited in several books related to spiritual leadership and organizational development.

Dr. Adelson was raised in the San Fernando Valley in Los Angeles, California and lived in both Northern and Southern California with his life partner and husband Thomas for 53 years before Thomas succumbed to Alzheimer's Disease in 2023. He currently resides in the Palm Springs area, where he is an active volunteer and advocate with the Alzheimer's Association, supporting caregivers and families whose loved ones are afflicted with this cruel disease.

Les Adelson

9 798330 286171